Measuring the outcomes of medical care

Papers based on a conference held in September 1989 organised
by the Royal College of Physicians and the King's Fund Centre
for Health Services Development

Edited by
Anthony Hopkins
Director, Research Unit, Royal College of Physicians
and Consultant Neurologist, St Bartholomew's Hospital, London

and

David Costain
Director, Acute Services Programme, King's Fund Centre for Health
Services Development, London

THE ROYAL COLLEGE OF PHYSICIANS OF LONDON

KING'S FUND CENTRE FOR HEALTH SERVICES DEVELOPMENT

Royal College of Physicians
11 St Andrews Place, London NW1 4LE

© 1990 Royal College of Physicians of London
ISBN 0 900596 97 X

Reprinted 1991

Reprinted 1993

Reprinted 1995

Typeset by Oxprint Ltd, Aristotle Lane, Oxford OX2 6TR
Printed by Antony Rowe Ltd, Bumpers Farm, Chippenham, Wiltshire SN14 6QA

Editors' introduction

The Royal College of Physicians and the King's Fund have both recently published reports on medical audit, which give useful guidance on how physicians may audit clinical records and the process of care. Such audit has been shown to improve record keeping and communication and may encourage a thoughtful use of resources. However, it tells nothing about the effectiveness of medical interventions, which must be shown to be effective in achieving a desired outcome in order to justify their continued use. Mortality is an insensitive measure of outcome, as many illnesses are fortunately not mortal. Without definition and measurement of other outcomes, the audit of process is an inadequate measure of the quality of medical care.

The Royal College of Physicians and the King's Fund held a one-day conference on 28 September 1989 at which these issues were explored. This volume is an edited version of the papers presented at the conference. The writers explore some of the important issues related to measurements of outcome. Professor Rachel Rosser describes the development of measures of health status and of the quality of life, and counsels us against too readily translating such measures into a prescription for health policy. Professor Shah Ebrahim gives a useful review of the measurement of impairment disability and handicap, and shows that, seen in those terms, medical intervention can still be effective even if the natural history of biological illness is not much altered. Dr Henry McQuay summarizes the ways in which pain can be measured, and makes a plea for the more widespread use of simple pain charts in everyday clinical care. Dr Ray Fitzpatrick, whilst recognising that patient satisfaction is irrelevant to the cure of disease, stresses just how important an outcome of care it is to have a patient who is happy with his treatment, and reviews the methodology for assessing this aspect of care. Professor David Metcalfe provides a helpful framework in which the outcomes of care in general practice can be measured by identifying simple objectives of care. Dr Robert Brook has been interested for many years in studying the appropriateness of medical interventions, but he here shows how difficult it is to relate appropriateness to outcome. Mr Jim Coles describes how refashioned performance indicators can be more useful in comparing outcomes between clinical units. Dr Paul Schyve, from the Joint Commission on Accreditation of

Health Care Organizations, shows how structural aspects of the provision of care are related to outcomes.

In order to justify the continued use of medical intervention, that intervention has to be shown to be effective. Medical audit of the effectiveness of care depends therefore entirely upon the measurement of outcomes. We hope that these collected papers will provide a useful introduction to the field.

ANTHONY HOPKINS
Research Unit,
Royal College of Physicians

DAVID COSTAIN
King's Fund Centre for
Health Services Development

Contributors

Robert H. Brook MD ScD *Chief, Division of Geriatrics; Professor of Medicine and of Public Health Medicine, UCLA Center for Social Sciences Department, and RAND Corporation, Santa Monica, California 90406, USA.*

Anthony W. Clare MD FRCPI FRCPsych *Clinical Professor of Psychiatry, Trinity College, Dublin and Medical Director, St Patrick's Hospital, Dublin 8, Republic of Ireland.*

James Coles MSc(Eng) *Associate Director, CASPE Research, King Edward's Hospital Fund for London, London W2 4HT.*

Shah Ebrahim DM MSc MRCP MRCGP MFCM *Joint Professor, Department of Health Care of the Elderly, The London and St Bartholomew's Hospital Medical Colleges, London E1 4DG.*

Ray Fitzpatrick BA MSc PhD *Fellow, Nuffield College, Oxford and University Lecturer in Medical Sociology, Department of Community Medicine and General Practice, University of Oxford.*

David H. H. Metcalfe OBE FRCGP FFCM *Professor, Department of General Practice, University of Manchester Rusholme Health Centre, Manchester M14 5NP.*

Henry J. McQuay DM *Clinical Reader in Pain Relief, University of Oxford, Oxford Regional Pain Relief Unit, Abingdon Hospital, Marsham Road, Abingdon, Oxon OX14 1AG.*

James S. Roberts MD *Senior Vice President, Joint Commission on Accreditation of Healthcare Organizations, Chicago, Illinois 60611, U.S.A.*

Rachel Rosser MB PhD FRCP FRCPsych *Professor and Head of Department of Academic Psychiatry, University College and Middlesex School of Medicine, Riding House Street, London W1N 8AA.*

Paul M. Schyve MD *Vice President for Research and Standards, Joint Commission on Healthcare Organizations, Chicago, Illinois 60611, U.S.A.*

Contents

1 | From health indicators to quality adjusted life years: technical and ethical issues

Rachel Rosser

Department of Academic Psychiatry, University College and Middlesex School of Medicine, London

The distinguished nineteenth century economist Alfred Marshall summarised a text of nearly 700 pages in a 16-page mathematical appendix.[1] The following 'health index formula'[2] attempts to do the same for my subject.

$$\sum_{t=0}^{l} [f_{ijt}(m_{it}) - f_{ijt}(m'_{it})] + \sum_{t=l+1}^{k} [D_{ijt} - f_{ijt}(m'_{it})]$$

This represents the difference in the utility, f, of the morbidity, m, experienced by the patient, i, after treatment (which is denoted by a prime) compared with the morbidity experienced without treatment during the natural and untreated lifespan, l. To this is added the difference between the utility of being dead (state D) after the time at which death would occur without treatment (k) compared with the utility of the morbidity experienced by the treated and therefore surviving patient between time $l + 1$ and time k.

The formula indicates that utility may be affected not only by the definition of morbidity state but also by the characteristics of the patient other than attributes of illness, eg age, occupation and marital status. It may also reflect characteristics of the judges who provide the valuation (shown by the term j); for example, the value systems of older judges may differ from those of the younger ones. In addition, the time, t, at which values are elicited may be important. Consider how attitudes have changed over the past 200 years to symptoms and conditions such as psychosexual difficulties, delusions, depression or cosmetic defects on the one hand, and coughs, fevers, bacterial infections and diabetes on the other. The formula provides a definition of the improvement in the morbidity of patient i as a result of the treatment received. It is an absolute measure and takes into account spontaneous deterioration and remission.[2]

The sum of the improvements in all patients treated by a medical service in a given period provides a measure of the output of the service during that period. In practice many of the elements thus defined, especially data relating to the natural history of treatable diseases, are not directly measurable and operational assumptions have to be made. However, this theoretical model provides the conceptual framework within which these assumptions may be judged.

The formula forms the basis of cross-diagnostic or global indices of health which were designed in the 1960s and 1970s for use in evaluating and planning services.[3] The pressure to broaden the concept to embrace the quality of life came from various sources, not least the political debate about the allocation of public funds between health and other activities intended to improve the population's quality of life (Fig. 1).

My colleagues have simplified the underlying logic with the help of graphs.[4] To understand Fig. 2, imagine an individual who has the advantage of experiencing perfect health and a maximum lifespan. That individual's life, terminated in sudden death, is shown as the frame of

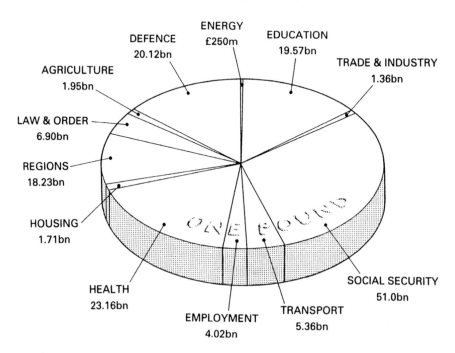

SLICING UP THE SPENDING CAKE

Where the money will go, 1989–90

Fig. 1. *Allocation of Gross National Product.* From *The Times*, 2 November 1988. © Times Newspapers Ltd.

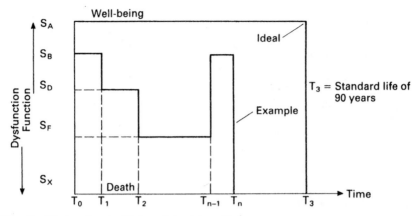

Fig. 2. *Ideal and typical lifetime's health profile.*[4]

this graph. Beneath is a diagram of a typical imperfect life, perhaps the lifetime illness profile of an individual suffering from a chronic and partially remediable condition such as diabetes or schizophrenia. Taking the example of diabetes, the pregnancy and birth may be somewhat complicated if the child is born of a diabetic mother and thus the initial state is less than ideal. Early in life diabetes is diagnosed as a consequence of sudden coma which would result in death, as indicated by the dashed lines, if treatment did not occur. On diet and insulin the child's quality of life is impaired and later complications set in. However, the development of improved insulin preparations, better understanding of the psychosocial needs of people with this condition, and technological advances for the treatment of complications such as retinopathy result in a substantial improvement in quality of life. Nonetheless, early death occurs from a subsequent complication.

A similar profile could describe the life of the child of a woman suffering from schizophrenia who is fostered, eventually develops schizophrenia, enters an institution, benefits from improvements in pharmacological and social treatment and is rehabilitated into the community, but dies prematurely perhaps from suicide or as a consequence of self-neglect.

Suppose that for a particular health district a new programme is introduced in which institutional containment for people with schizophrenic illnesses is replaced by a comprehensive community programme drawing on all modern treatment techniques. The gap between the dashed line labelled 'well-being' at the top of Fig. 3 and the bottom line labelled 'without programme' indicates the loss of quality of life of this population without the new treatment programme. It could be said that each year of life of those people with schizophrenia has a lower value

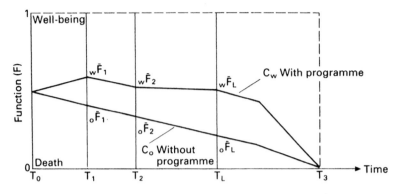

Fig. 3. *Effect on health states of disease and of treatment programme.*[4]

than the life of a healthy person and the gap could be calculated as the sum of the life years effectively lost because of this discrepancy in quality. The curve between the two lines labelled 'with programme' and 'without programme' provides a measure of the benefit due to these services expressed in quality adjusted life years gained on average by each member of the target population. This can be related to service cost. Such a cost-utility analysis is being conducted in collaboration with Professor Isaac Marks (Institute of Psychiatry) and Professor Martin Knapp (Department of Economics, University of Kent). It entails a randomised standard controlled trial of a 'daily living programme' for severe mental illness.[5]

In this paper I plan to show how these abstract equations and diagrams are converted into operational measures. I shall try to expose the logical assumptions at each step and give an up-to-date account of the empirical support for these. I shall demonstrate that the transition from an index of quality of life to cost-per-QALY league tables entails an ethical sleight of hand. The emphasis in my group is gradually shifting from work in the technical area to a study of the philosophical basis for the use of these measures and the extent to which they are culture-bound. I shall draw on the work of our group and close colleagues throughout the world.[6]

Global indices of health

The original formula specifies a system for describing states of morbidity, m, and a scale which assigns to each a relative value or utility, f.

Our first descriptive system is shown in Table 1. This was derived by asking 60 doctors of various levels of seniority and various specialties about the criteria they used, leaving aside prognosis and diagnosis, in

Table 1. Original descriptions of disability and distress[7]

Disability	Distress
1. No disability	1. None
2. Not in 3 but slight social disability	2. Mild
3. Not in 4 but severe social disability and/or slight impairment of performance at work. Able to do all housework except very heavy tasks.	3. Moderate 4. Severe
4. Not in 5 but choice of work or performance at work severely limited. Housewives and old people able to do light housework only, but able to go out shopping.	
5. Not in 6 but unable to undertake any paid employment. Unable to continue any education. Old people confined to home except for escorted outings and short walks and unable to do shopping. Housewives only unable to perform a few simple tasks.	
6. Not in 7 but confined to chair or wheelchair or able to move around in the home only with support from an assistant.	
7. Not in 8 but confined to bed.	
8. Unconscious.	

Notes on definitions of disability

This describes the extent to which a patient is judged to be unable to pursue the activities of a normal person at the time at which the classification is made. Patients in Class 2 are slightly disabled, but performance in their normal work is not impaired. This degree of disablement affects social activities and personal relationships. It includes such conditions as mild cosmetic defects, slight injuries and diseases which may interfere with hobbies but not with essential activities, and some of the less severe psychiatric states which cause some social disablement.

Notes on definitions of distress

This describes the patient's pain, mental suffering in relation to disablement, anxiety and depression.

	Pain	*Mental disturbance*
State 1	None	No mental distress
State 2	The patient has mild pain such as that of mild toothache for which analgesics such as aspirin might be prescribed.	Mild mental distress
State 3	The patient has moderate pain, eg severe migraine-type headache.	Moderate mental distress
State 4	The patient has severe pain, eg due to subarachnoid haemorrhage. Pains for which morphine might be prescribed.	Severe mental distress

Table 2. DGH study: percentage of patients in each morbidity state on admission[9]

	Distress			
Disability	1	2	3	4
1	19	12	3	1
2	10	12	3	1
3	1	3	1	1
4	3	3	5	1
5	1	3	4	2
6	1	1	2	0
7	1	2	3	1
8	0	0	0	0

judging the severity of one person's state relative to another. We identified eight states of disability (including unconsciousness) and four levels of distress, giving 29 possible combinations. This system of classification proved highly reliable in intra-observer and test/re-test situations with doctors, nurses and multi-disciplinary teams.[7,8]

We applied this system to all inpatients and outpatients of a district general hospital (DGH) during a survey period of 1 month, resulting in more than 2,000 classifications.[9] Similar studies have been done over the years but I will draw on these early data because they happen to illustrate the points I need to make.

Table 2 shows the percentage distribution of states of patients on admission. By chance, no patients were admitted in the unconscious state during the month of the study. Note that 19% of patients were admitted free of disability and distress either for elective surgery or for investigations or treatment which could have an effect on prognosis but not on immediate symptoms. A similar study 6 years later in a London teaching hospital showed that only 3% of patients were admitted in this state, and recent data show figures of less than 1%. It is very difficult in 1989 to gain admission to a London hospital without significant symptoms!

Table 3 shows the distribution of states at discharge. There has been an overall movement from the bottom right to the top left of the matrix; 33% of patients are now free of disability and distress while 1% have severe distress. The distributions are statistically significantly different.

Table 3. DGH study: percentage distribution at discharge[9]

Disability	Distress			
	1	2	3	4
1	33	10	1	0
2	21	11	1	0
3	2	3	1	0
4	3	4	1	0
5	3	2	2	1
6	0	0	1	0
7	0	0	0	0
8	0	0	0	0

There has been a considerable relief of disability and distress whether by spontaneous remission or because of treatment.

To apply this technique it is necessary to define an episode of care; for a physician an inpatient stay may be an appropriate definition but for a surgeon convalescence tends to occur at home and the first follow-up visit is a more appropriate end-point.

Table 4 shows the situation at first outpatient follow-up visit. The conclusion is now more ambiguous: 45% of patients are free of disability

Table 4. DGH study: percentage distribution at first outpatient attendance after discharge[9]

Disability	Distress			
	1	2	3	4
1	45	7	0	0
2	7	11	2	0
3	3	4	2	0
4	1	2	2	0
5	2	8	1	0
6	1	1	1	0
7	0	0	0	0
8	0	0	0	0

and distress. This represents a considerable improvement on the previous figure of 33%. Nonetheless, a few patients have deteriorated and some of the cells indicating greater disability and distress are now occupied. Although this distribution is statistically significantly different from the other two (Tables 2 and 3) it is no longer possible to say at first glance whether the distribution of scores at outpatient follow-up represents on balance an improvement or a deterioration compared with that at discharge. For that purpose it is necessary to make a judgement about whether the improvement in a considerable proportion of patients is more or less offset by the deterioration in a minority. For this purpose a scale is needed which places a value, f, on every state relative to every other state.

Table 5 illustrates such a scale derived from 4-hour psychometric interviews with 70 people having different personal and professional experiences of illness and health. The scale was derived by the method of magnitude estimation and has the following features.[10] First, death is not the worst possible state. People view permanent unconsciousness or confinement to bed in severe pain or depression as even more undesirable than death. Second, there is a diagonal relationship between states so that people are willing to trade off between disability and distress; this is consistent with the clinical practices of bed-rest and sedation on the one hand and active rehabilitation on the other. Third, the range of the scale is much greater than that which would be obtained by simply ranking the 29 states. Indeed, we have shown with many applied studies that scales based on simple ranking rules lead to different

Table 5.   Geometric mean scale derived by magnitude estimation[7]

	Distress			
Disability	1	2	3	4
1	—	0.25	1.36	10.70
2	0.56	1.32	3.67	19.66
3	2.25	4.14	7.39	40.56
4	5.01	10.08	14.98	58.95
5	7.83	10.67	20.66	88.40
6	21.39	29.21	79.44	218.58
7	83.44	110.01	306.20	804.07
8	812.61			

Death = 210.

conclusions from psychometric scales which are themselves broadly consistent regardless of how they are elicited and statistically analysed.[7]

When these scale values were applied to the admission and follow-up states of every patient in the DGH study we found that, for the major specialties, the improvement from admission to discharge represented 66% of what could theoretically be achieved if all patients became free of disability and distress. This figure is meaningless on its own but becomes more informative when this hospital is compared with others working under similar conditions.

It is also interesting to compare the performance of different components of the hospital service, again operating under similar conditions. In Table 6 seven teams are shown, all admitting predominantly emergencies from the same community. One medical and one surgical firm are academic firms with a lower sessional input from the consultants and thus should perhaps be compared with one another rather than with the larger firms. But a comparison of the medical teams and of the surgical teams is of great interest. The table shows that the ranking of teams by throughput of patients is quite different from the ranking by impact on disability and distress.

The question then arises as to how these data might be used in practice. Our group has suggested that they should be collected by the profession and made available at clinical audit meetings. Clinical policies could then be reviewed to see whether they could be adjusted so as to improve the output of the units. For example, it became clear that one of the physicians in this study was particularly gifted in determining the length of stay of his patients. They remained in hospital slightly longer than average but did not deteriorate between discharge and first outpatient visit. Another physician, keen to improve throughput, was possibly discharging prematurely. Similarly, one of the surgeons, also enthusiastic about service statistics, tended to admit large numbers of mild cases in whom little improvement could be achieved. For him the recommendation would be to confine the treatment of these people to day care and use inpatient services for the more severely ill.

Over the years several studies have been done on my own wards and these have led me to examine more carefully what can be achieved in treating people with combined physical and psychiatric disorder, with personality disorder underlying a formal psychiatric illness, and those with psychogenic pain and other disproportionate and intractable somatic symptoms.

Such data may be useful but they are clearly open to abuse. There is concern about managerial interference with clinical decisions. What about the needs of the chronically ill, the old, and those in terminal care?

As more technical and ethical assumptions are made, the potential

Table 6. DGH study: effect on present states (EPS) of patients for one month of seven units. From Rosser, R.M. (1976)

Unit	(1) N = patients treated	(2) Total score on admission	(3) Total score at first outpatient visit after discharge	(4) EPS	(5) EPS as percentage of potential EPS	(6) EPS as percentage of total
		(a)	(b)	(a−b)		
Surgery 1	33	438	206	232	53.0	9.2
Surgery 2	23	600	117	483	80.5	19.1
Surgery 3	8	115	49	66	57.4	2.6
Internal medicine 1	28	607	590	17	2.8	0.7
Internal medicine 2	37	1,162	93	1,069	92.0	42.2
Internal medicine 3	5	245	111	134	54.7	5.3
Psychiatry	29	615	84	531	86.3	20.9
Total EPS for this group of clinicians	163	3,782	1,250	2,532	66.9	100.0

Potential EPS = maximum possible EPS achievable if all disability and distress could be completely relieved (column 4 as percentage of column 2).

for abuse grows.[11] The next step also involves some linguistic licence; the global index of health is transformed into a method for measuring quality adjusted life years by a mere mathematical device!

Quality adjusted life years

Tables 7 and 8 show the scale of disability and distress at different stages of standardisation. First, using the median magnitude estimations, the interval between the first and second states, namely freedom from

Table 7. Median scale with first interval set at 1[7]

Disability	Distress			
	1	2	3	4
1	0	1.00	2.00	6.67
2	2.00	2.70	5.45	13.50
3	4.00	5.53	8.75	17.50
4	7.25	8.70	11.67	26.00
5	10.85	13.03	20.00	60.00
6	25.00	31.00	64.00	200.00
7	64.50	87.20	200.00	497.14
8	405.71			

Table 8. Utility scale for QALY calculations[12]

Disability	Distress			
	1	2	3	4
1	1.00	0.96	0.99	0.97
2	0.99	0.99	0.97	0.93
3	0.98	0.97	0.96	0.91
4	0.96	0.96	0.94	0.87
5	0.95	0.94	0.90	0.70
6	0.88	0.85	0.68	0.00
7	0.68	0.56	0.00	–1.49
8	–1.03			

disability and distress and freedom from disability with slight distress,
is set at 1. The other intervals are adjusted accordingly.

Then the scale is inverted so that freedom from disability and distress
is assigned a value of 1, death is assigned a value of 0 and permanent
states which are worse than death receive negative values.[12]

The final stages are as follows. In the absence of accurate prospective
epidemiological data on the quality adjusted life years experienced by
patients in treated and untreated disease states, economists at the
University of York elicited judgements from clinicians about the likely
lifetime profiles of quality of life with and without treatment. Then the
benefit of quality adjusted life years (QALYs) is divided by the cost of
treatment to produce a league table of treatments in terms of the costs
of each QALY they produce (Table 9).[13–15]

However, it must be realised that at some unspecified point some
economists have departed from the realm of technical approximation
and made assumptions of a different kind requiring a philosophical
defence. It is implied that the point of these tables is to enable the health

Table 9. Cost-per-QALY league table[14]

	QALYs gained per patient (discounted at 5%)	Annual cost per patient (£s)	Total cost (discounted at 5%) (£s)	Cost per QALY (£s)
Continuous ambulatory peritoneal dialysis (4 years)	3.4	12,866	45,676	13,434[a]
Haemodialysis (8 years)	6.1	8,569	55,354	9,075[a]
Treatment of cystic fibrosis with ceftazidime (over 22 years)	0.4	250	3,290	8,225[a]
Kidney transplant (lasting 10 years)	7.4	10,452	10,452	1,413[b]
Shoulder joint replacement (lasting 10 years)	0.9	533	533	592[b]
Scoliosis surgery idiopathic adolescent	1.2	3,143	3,143	2,619[b]
neuromuscular illness	16.2	3,143	3,143	194[b]

[a] Represents recurring annual costs and annual QALYs per case.
[b] Represents one-off costs per case, and benefits discounted over life of case.

service to achieve the delivery of the maximum output in QALYs in return for a fixed amount of expenditure. If taken at face value, it appears that there is a danger that certain treatments such as chronic ambulatory peritoneal dialysis might cease, resulting in the death of those for whom no other treatment is appropriate, whilst the use of other treatments such as pacemakers might increase.

These bold steps were taken rather rapidly. Let us go back and scrutinise some of the technical and ethical assumptions which underlie them.

Technical assumptions

Table 10 lists some of the more obvious technical assumptions.[16] These are of concern to clinicians and to more cautious economists.[17,18] Data from our group cast doubt on the validity of every one of them (Butler, Rabin and Rosser, to be published). Disability and distress do retain their position as important descriptors in all our studies. We have recently divided distress, separating 5 levels of pain from 5 levels of mental distress, increasing the possible number of states from 29 to 175. Furthermore, our population surveys have demonstrated that there are many other descriptors of ill health which may be rated even when people declare themselves to be free of disability, distress and pain. These may not make a substantial difference to the final utility scale but the comprehensiveness of the descriptive system should be kept under review. We also find that the passage of time is not perceived in a linear manner and this needs to be taken into account when calculating QALY benefits of treatments for conditions of different duration. The QALY method in present use discounts future illness at an annual rate of 5% but we find that nowadays, in contrast with 10 years ago, future illness is not discounted. (This is consistent with the growing response to health education, screening and primary preventive measures.) We also find

Table 10. Technical assumptions

---

1. Description: validity/comprehensiveness

2. Scaling: consistency of method/aggregation of data/source of data

3. Validity of index: absence of criterion

4. Time: duration/discounting into future

5. Outcome data: prospectively measured/judgemental

6. Linearity of scale permits division by resources, also measured on linear scale

---

that, although there is consistency in the scale values produced by people from different ages and social backgrounds, there is substantial variation in the scales produced by people with different personal and professional experiences of ill health.

Finally, our data cast doubt on the assumption of linearity. We find that the magnitude method of utility measurement yields a scale which bears a log-linear relationship to other psychometric techniques[19] (Butler and Rosser, submitted). We now prefer to use either the 'standard gamble'[19a] or various forms of category rating. We are also re-assessing the method of paired comparisons and other classical approaches.[20]

As a consequence, we have designed a more elaborate instrument, the index of health-related quality of life (IHQL) with more than a hundred descriptors which subsume the original classification of disability, pain and distress. Scales, attributes and dimensions can be valued separately or combined to produce a single IHQL score. Calculations can also be corrected for states of different duration. We are using the IHQL to collect prospective data in a number of clinical settings covering psychiatric and acute medical and surgical services. This will enable us to examine the validity of quantified expert judgement as a substitute for prospective objective data (Allison and Rosser, to be published).

Ethical assumptions

The philosophical assumption underlying the use of cost-per-QALY league tables is utilitarian. Writing from the home of Jeremy Bentham, I regret that I cannot give this my unreserved support! It may be argued that the health service budget must be used to give the greatest good to the greatest number; it follows that the cheapest cost-per-QALY treatments will result in the maximum possible number of QALYs being spread amongst the population. This axiom causes me concern. I had imagined that the measure I derived would be used to quantify the consequences of decisions so that planners and policy-makers could debate clinical and ethical issues free of uncertainty about the impact of their decisions on the outcome of treatment. In practice the very opposite seems to be happening, and the measure seems to be offered as a way of circumventing such debates, as if it can do our thinking for us.

If one does not accept the utilitarian hard line, must one reject the measurement of quality of life? I do not think so. I suggest that the appropriate uses of QALY calculations and, indeed, cost-per-QALY league tables may be entirely different. Health authorities should consider how to make use of the accurate data available. A wide range of decisions might emerge after discussion from different authorities. Some possible decisions might be:

It is unacceptable in a civilised society that anybody should linger in a treatable condition judged to be worse than death. Resources will be set aside for the care and treatment of all people in such states.

or Resources will be allocated in rank order to people with the poorest present or the poorest lifetime expectancy of quality of life.

or Low-cost per QALY treatments will be marketed (through the internal or private market) and high-cost per QALY treatments will be protected either as core services or as new developments.

or Services will be divided into those that are at most ameliorative and those that are curative, and comparisons will only occur within these groups.

or Innovatory and expensive treatments will be regarded as applied research; their costs per QALY will be monitored but initially they will not compete with established treatments.

or There will be no single policy but cost-per-QALY data will be used for continuous audit and planning, and the underlying ethical and philosophical issues will be discussed at every review.

Many alternatives are possible.

Interdependence of technical and ethical issues

In this paper, a distinction has been drawn between technical assumptions, amenable to empirical investigation, on the one hand[21] and philosophical and ethical assumptions, requiring rigorous logical analysis, on the other. This is, of course, an oversimplification, since there is an interplay between these two areas of discourse which has an immediate impact on the research–policy cycle.[16] The semantic definition of quality of life, its representation by a linear model, the concept of utility, the underlying theory of measurement, aggregation of values across groups of individuals, principles of fairness and desert, are all matters requiring both philosophical and technical examination. Ultimately, the metaphysical assumption that freedom from disability, pain and suffering is desirable is not irrefutable, being but one manifestation of the Western transient and materialistic frame of reference. (For an analysis of some of these issues, see Refs 22 and 23.)

Conclusion

Measurement of the utility of health-related quality of life and its improvement during treatment offers a method of informing health service decisions about the values of users, providers and tax-payers. It supplements both traditional measures of service activity and political processes of responding to public opinion. However, if the methodology is not technically robust and is applied so as to pre-empt ethical debate, it will serve to reduce rather than raise the standards of clinical care.

Acknowledgement

This research has been supported by grants from the Department of Health and Social Security since 1969.

References

1. Marshall, A. (1890) *Principles of economics*. London: Macmillan.
2. Rosser, R.M. and Watts, V.C. (1978) The measurement of illness. *Journal of Operational Research*, **29**, 529–40.
3. Torrance, G.W. (1976) Health index and utility models: a unified mathematical view. *Management Science*, **22**, 990–1001.
4. Fanshel, S. and Bush J.W. (1970) A health status index and its application to health service outcomes. *Operations Research*, **18**, 1021–66.
5. Marks, I., Connolly, J. and Muirjen, M. (1988) The Maudsley daily living programme: a controlled cost-effectiveness study of community-based versus standard in-patient care of serious mental illness. *Bulletin of the Royal College of Psychiatrists*, **12**(1), 22–4.
6. Walker, S.R. and Rosser, R.M. (eds) (1988) *Quality of life: assessment and application*. Lancaster: MTP Press.
7. Rosser, R.M. (1980) A set of descriptions and a psychometric scale of severity of illness: an indicator for use in evaluating the outcome of hospital care. PhD thesis. University of London.
8. Benson, T.J.R. (1978) Classification of disability and distress by ward nurses: a reliability study. *International Journal of Epidemiology*, **7**, 359–61.
9. Rosser, R.M. and Watts, V.C. (1972) The measurement of hospital output. *International Journal of Epidemiology*, **1**, 361–8.
10. Rosser, R.M. and Kind, P. (1978) A scale of valuations of states of illness — Is there a social consensus? *International Journal of Epidemiology*, **7**, 347–58.
11. Klein, R. (1989) The role of health economics. *British Medical Journal*, **299**, 275–6.
12. Kind, P., Rosser, R.M. and Williams, A. (1982) Valuation of quality of life: some psychometric evidence. In *The value of life and safety* (ed. M.W. Jones-Lee) pp 159–70. Amsterdam: North-Holland.
13. Williams, A. (1985) Economics of coronary artery bypass grafting. *British Medical Journal*, **291**, 736–7.
14. Gudex, C. (1986) QALYs and their use by the health service. University of York Centre for Health Economics. Discussion paper No. 20.
15. Williams, A. (1988) The importance of quality of life in policy decisions. In *Quality of life* (see Ref. 6) pp 279–90.
16. Rosser, R.M. (1988) Quality of life: consensus, controversy and concern. In *Quality of life* (see Ref. 6) pp 297–304.
17. Drummond, M. (1987) Resource allocation decisions in health care: a role for quality of life assessments? *Journal of Chronic Diseases*, **40**(6), 606–16.
18. McDonnell, R. and Maynard, A. (1985) Estimation of life years lost from alcohol-related premature death. *Alcohol and Alcoholism*, **20**(4), 435–43.
19. Kind, P. and Rosser, R.M. (1988) The quantification of health. *European Journal of Social Psychology*, **18**, 63–77.

19a. Neumann, J. von and Morgenstern, D. (1953)· *Theory of games and economic behaviour* (3rd edn). New York: Wiley.

20. Fishbein, R. (1967) *Readings in attitude theory and measurement.* New York: John Wiley & Sons.

21. Rosser, R.M. (1983) Issues of measurement in the design of health indicators: a review. In *Health indicators* (ed. A.J. Culyer) pp 34–81. Amsterdam: North-Holland Biomedical Press.

22. Griffin, J.G. (1986) *Well being: its meaning, measurement, and moral importance.* Oxford: Clarendon Press.

23. Smith, A. (1987) Qualms about QALYs. *Lancet,* **i,** 1134–6.

2 | Measurement of patient satisfaction

Ray Fitzpatrick
Department of Community Medicine and General Practice, University of Oxford

Recent developments outside the National Health Service (NHS) have made the inclusion of clients' or consumers' assessment of services a more salient issue. Social trends such as consumerism and the growing importance of market research in commercial decision-making have both played a part. Public sector services have necessarily become more accountable and responsive to consumers' preferences. Within the NHS these general currents gained specific and influential expression in the Griffiths NHS management inquiry. A key conclusion of the report was that the NHS had failed to demonstrate sufficient responsiveness to consumers and that it needed to invest more effort in obtaining systematic evidence of patients' satisfaction. Since the report, there has been an unprecedented flurry of activity as Health Authorities have rushed to show their commitment to eliciting the consumer's viewpoint. A recent study[1] found that all but one Region in the NHS had produced policy documents on quality assurance and customer relations, and all had a Regional officer with responsibilities in this area. The vast majority of Districts were in a similar position. Surveys of patient satisfaction appeared to be key components of all of this activity.

Despite the emphasis placed upon patient satisfaction by recent trends within NHS management, serious reservations about the value of patients' views remain. It is worth briefly considering the arguments for and against patient satisfaction surveys. Patient satisfaction is an outcome measure, and provides an important alternative assessment of the results of health care. Many authoritative discussions of the evaluation of health care include consumers' views as a central component.[2,3] They are included in Maxwell's list[4] of the six dimensions of quality of medical care: access, relevance to need, effectiveness, equity, efficiency and *social acceptability*. However, there are important respects in which patient satisfaction is unlike other measures of outcome, and serious reservations have often been expressed about its use in this context.[5,6]

More specific arguments for using patients' views in the evaluation of health care need to be briefly stated. The first and most general argument has already been implied by our reference to the Griffiths inquiry. According to this view, consumers of public services should participate as far as is reasonable in setting the standards for the services which are ultimately funded by them and which are there to serve their needs. This verges on an argument for citizens' rights.[7] A second argument is that for many aspects of health care, such as personal care, giving information, accessibility to care and pleasantness of facilities, it is hard to conceive of omitting the consumers' views, in the absence of alternative indicators of quality. In terms of Donabedian's framework for evaluating health care, it may be more accurate to think of patient satisfaction in this context as a 'process' measure rather than an 'outcome' measure. It measures how well services are provided, rather than the results (outcome) of services. The third argument is based on research evidence that suggests that patient satisfaction makes a direct contribution to other outcomes that are of undoubted importance to medical care. Thus patients who are more dissatisfied with their care are more likely not to comply with medical advice,[8,9] not to reattend the particular service for further treatment,[10] and may even be less likely to show improvement in symptoms.[11]

The arguments against using measures of patient satisfaction in health service research can be traced to four kinds of reservations which I consider below. They concern questions about (i) the proper scope and competence of patients to judge technical medical care, (ii) the factors that influence patients' views, (iii) the reliability and validity of instruments to assess patient satisfaction and (iv) the practical utility of survey results. Many problems in research however stem from a failure to examine the concept of satisfaction.

What is meant by patient satisfaction?

In view of the amount of effort that is currently being invested in conducting surveys of patient satisfaction in this country and elsewhere, it would be reasonable to expect that the concept of satisfaction had been clearly defined and that some effort had been made to measure the phenomenon with a degree of consistency. This is far from the case. Patient satisfaction is one of those concepts that has a common-sense meaning which is rarely subject to critical scrutiny. It is sometimes treated as an attitude or set of attitudes but is more usefully thought of as an evaluation or set of evaluations by the patient. Pascoe[12] regards patient satisfaction as involving a *cognitive evaluation* of health care and an *emotional reaction* to health care. The proliferation of different ways of measuring satisfaction partly arises out of the diversity of health care

settings which have been examined but also stems from central un-
certainties as to the scope of the concept.

Patients evaluate their health care on a number of different and
separate aspects. How many dimensions patients distinguish in their
evaluations of care is not universally agreed but several studies assess
patients' views separately on each of the following dimensions: personal
aspects of care, technical quality of care, accessibility and availability
of care, continuity of care, acceptability and convenience of physical
setting, and effectiveness of treatment. In American but not British
surveys a distinct dimension of financial costs is normally identified.[13]
According to this approach it is wrong to assume a global or overall level
of satisfaction. Different dimensions of views are distinct and do not
necessarily correlate with each other. Global measures of satisfaction
may reflect a variety of influences upon the patient that cannot easily be
disentangled. However, some reports suggest that dimensions cannot
be statistically distinguished. In particular, it is suggested that patients
do not have distinct evaluations of the personal and the technical aspects
of professional care.[14]

Scope of surveys of patient satisfaction

One central problem concerns the proper scope of patient satisfaction
surveys. We can all think of instances of the patient who was remarkably
impressed by treatment which in professional medical terms was poor.
Such instances provoke general unease about the boundaries of patient
satisfaction research. Can there be any value in obtaining feedback from
patients in regard to technical, medical aspects of treatment, which
require high levels of technical competence to evaluate? Most patients
do not have this level of competence. In practice most patient satisfaction
research acknowledges this problem by examining patients' views in
multidimensional terms. Questions about the content of treatment are
conceived of as but one specific dimension alongside judgements of
interpersonal aspects of care, accessibility of care, views about information, and so on. It has been shown that views about these other aspects
of treatment are independent of views about the technical quality of care
received. Those who are anxious about the competence of patients to
contribute to evaluation should be reassured by this multidimensional
approach to measurement.

Reliability and validity of patient satisfaction questionnaires

There are two main ways of examining the reliability of any survey
instrument such as a patient satisfaction questionnaire. One way is to

examine the extent to which there is agreement between questionnaire items considered to be measuring the same construct. The second approach, test–retest reliability, assesses the extent of agreement between responses to a questionnaire at two different times. Overall it must be said that little attention has been given to these aspects of patient satisfaction questionnaires. In the exceptional circumstances where instruments have been carefully developed and subject to inter-item reliability tests, the results have been encouraging. However, one problem in interpreting these studies is that patients tend to express high levels of satisfaction with most items. In these circumstances it is difficult to have confidence in correlations between items as a measure of reliability. Very few instruments have been examined for test–retest reliability. The few unusually meticulous studies[8] that have considered this aspect of patient satisfaction research have generally found satisfactory levels of reliability.

There are enormous problems with establishing the validity of patient satisfaction questionnaires. It is hard to conceive of ways of checking whether answers given to questionnaires reflect respondents' true views. A more indirect approach is to examine 'construct validity'—the extent to which relationships between measures conform to theoretical predictions. One or two elegant studies have contributed to our understanding in this way. Stiles *et al.*[15] showed that patients' satisfaction with their consultations in an outpatient clinic were related to particular styles of communication used by the doctor. Patients were more satisfied with consultations in which they were encouraged by the doctor to explain their problems in their own terms. Other studies have related satisfaction to independent assessments of the quality and amount of information given to patients in consultations.[16]

Factors influencing patient satisfaction

Social and demographic variables have been shown to influence patient satisfaction. Unfortunately these effects are inconsistent between studies. Younger patients tend to report more dissatisfaction than older patients. In some surveys men express more dissatisfaction than women. Middle class and more highly educated patients may also express more dissatisfaction. The effects of these demographic variables are partly due to differences in readiness to express negative comments in response to questionnaires and partly represent more fundamental differences in expectations of health care. There is also evidence from some studies that patients with poorer health status or poorer mental health are more dissatisfied with their health care.[17] The effect of demographic variables makes the design and analysis of patient satisfaction surveys quite difficult. If, as is normally likely to be the case, the main purpose is to evaluate views of a particular service or one service compared with another, then much of the variance in patients' responses may be determined by extraneous (demographic) factors of no direct interest to the study.

What may be termed 'normative effects' may have widespread consequences upon the results of studies on patient satisfaction, although they may be difficult to demonstrate systematically. In an in-depth study of patients' evaluations of neurological clinics, a minority of patients were quite seriously disappointed by their clinic visit.[18] They nevertheless felt a number of pressures that they cited as reasons why they could not describe themselves as 'dissatisfied'. For some it was simply wrong to appear to be critical or unappreciative either of doctors or of the NHS. Others felt that the problems that had arisen in the clinic might have arisen from their own nervousness or diffidence about expressing their needs. These normative effects may be partly responsible for the high levels of satisfaction found in most surveys.

Practical utility of patient satisfaction surveys

A number of possible limitations of patient satisfaction surveys have already been discussed. In particular, responses may reflect the characteristics of patients rather than significant aspects of the provision of health care. However, there are other problems that still confront the investigator. Perhaps the single most difficult problem is that surveys often produce only modest amounts of variation because most patients— more than 85% in many surveys—are satisfied. It is difficult to attribute small variations to any significant aspect of service provision.

A different kind of problem arises from a lack of consideration of how one intends to use the information gained from a survey. Little consideration is generally given to the issues of *comparisons* and *consequences*. Commonly, a single 'snap-shot' survey is conducted and, particularly where the investigators have developed their own questionnaire, it becomes apparent that there is nothing with which to compare the results. A particular level of satisfaction obtained from a single sample has no intrinsic meaning. The problem of consequences is related to that of comparisons. Little thought is given to actions that may follow from obtaining patients' views. Staff are understandably frustrated if considerable effort has been put into gathering patients' views about a particular service and nothing seems to happen with the results. A recent analysis of customer relations surveys in the NHS appeared to conclude that many surveys were essentially public relations exercises.[1] Clinical Accountability, Service, Planning and Evaluation (CASPE) Research has developed patient satisfaction questionnaires for use in hospitals.[19] It aimed to overcome problems of comparisons by assessing mean satisfaction scores for the same units at regular intervals over time. It has tackled the problem of consequences by putting effort into involving management in the design of the questionnaire and in feeding back results quickly to the most appropriate unit.

Instruments to assess patient satisfaction

The vast majority of surveys are conducted with questionnaires completed by the patients because they are easier and cheaper to administer than interviews and produce unambiguous results. The specific format adopted in patient satisfaction questionnaires varies considerably. Unfortunately most surveys develop their own instruments with little reference to other studies. No questionnaire has yet been produced on the basis of sufficient developmental work to command authority in the field.

The simplest questionnaires ask individuals a question with 'yes' and 'no' as alternative answers, eg Was the treatment you received from the clinic helpful? (Yes/No).

This format leaves respondents with too small a range of choices to reflect their views. Frequently, the following format is therefore used: How helpful was the treatment you received from the hospital? (Very helpful/Quite helpful/Neither helpful nor unhelpful/Quite unhelpful/Very unhelpful).

One very different format tries to use more natural expressions that might normally be used to express views about health care. The item that follows is taken from a questionnaire produced by Dr A. Thompson when based at the University of Manchester Institute of Science and Technology. The questionnaire focuses on inpatient experiences and is one of the few instruments that has been widely used:[20]

> Prior to my admission to hospital, the information I was given about the reason I was admitted: left me very much in the dark; was rather sketchy on many details; gave a very full picture although I would have appreciated a little more; left no shadow of doubt in my mind.

In other areas of social research, scales are widely used which combine a number of items rather than rely on one question for each underlying construct. This is done to increase the reliability of measurement.[21] There are a few patient satisfaction questionnaires that adopt this approach by providing scales for each of a number of different dimensions of care (interpersonal, technical quality, effectiveness etc). However, such instruments tend to be confined to use in academic health service research. One reason for this may be that the results produced by a scale do not have the same intuitively understood and simple meaning that a single item permits. It is not possible to give a direct and simple statement of what percentage were satisfied or dissatisfied with a particular issue. A compromise between questionnaires with single questions for each domain and more elaborate scaling techniques is provided by the CASPE project's questionnaire. The answers to 15 different questions on various aspects of care are summed to produce one overall scale.

Interviews

There are alternatives to the questionnaire which should be considered. In particular, structured or semi-structured interviews have an important role to play. The advantage of such techniques is that it is possible to identify much more clearly the concerns and problems that patients face and how important to them are both their positive and negative evaluations.[18] A great limitation with all questionnaires is that all items receive equal weighting, but to the patient particular issues may vary enormously in significance, a distinction readily detected by interview. The disadvantages of the interview are principally that it is expensive and there are more problems than with a questionnaire of standardising the information obtained.

Conclusion

The use of patient satisfaction in the evaluation of health services has a longer and more productive history in the United States than in Britain. This partly reflects the greater diversity of institutional forms of providing care in the US and somewhat more direct market incentives to obtain consumers' views. Not surprisingly, most effort has gone into obtaining consumer feedback in relation to alternative ways of providing care, particularly comparisons of health maintenance organisations and more traditional fee for service options.[22] As we undergo a variety of institutional changes in the NHS, there are opportunities to incorporate consumers' views on their care and on the changes. Researchers are only now beginning to include the consumer's perceptions of the benefits of medical treatment.[23] The patient is not well placed to comment on the technical competence of health professionals, but he can certainly have views on the effects of care upon his health status. We need to make further efforts in improving our methodology of obtaining and measuring patients' perceptions of their care.

References

1. McIver, S. and Carr-Hill, R. (1989) *The NHS and its customers*. York: Centre for Health Economics.
2. Doll, R. (1973) Monitoring the National Health Service. *Proceedings of the Royal Society of Medicine*, **66**, 729–40.
3. Donabedian, A. (1988) The quality of care: how can it be assessed? *Journal of the American Medical Association*, **260**, 1743–8.
4. Maxwell, R. (1984) Quality assessment in health. *British Medical Journal*, **288**, 1470–2.
5. Marsh, G. and Kaim-Caudle, P. (1976) *Team care in general practice*. London: Croom Helm.
6. Mourin, K. and Mourin, M. (1986) Approaches to performance review: a review. In *In pursuit of quality* (ed. D. Pendleton, T. Schofield and M. Marinker). Devon: Royal College of General Practitioners.
7. Pollitt, C. (1988) Bringing consumers into performance measurement. *Policy and Politics*, **16**, 77–87.
8. Korsch, B., Gozzi, E. and Francis, V. (1968) Gaps in doctor–patient communications. 1. Doctor–patient interaction and patient satisfaction. *Paediatrics*, **42**, 855–71.
9. Fitzpatrick, R. and Hopkins, A. (1981) Patients' satisfaction with communication in neurological outpatient clinics. *Journal of Psychosomatic Research*, **25**, 329–34.
10. Roghmann, K., Hengst, A. and Zastowny, T. (1979) Satisfaction with medical care: its measurement and relation to utilisation. *Medical Care*, **17**, 461–77.
11. Fitzpatrick, R., Hopkins, A. and Harvard-Watts, O. (1983) Social dimensions of healing: a longitudinal study of outcomes of medical management of headaches. *Social Science and Medicine*, **17**, 501–10.
12. Pascoe, G. (1983) Patient satisfaction in primary health care: a literature review and analysis. *Evaluation and Program Planning*, **6**, 185–210.
13. Cleary, P. and McNeil, B. (1988) Patient satisfaction as an indicator of quality care. *Inquiry*, **25**, 25–36.
14. Ben Sira, Z. (1980) Affective and instrumental components in the physician–patient relationship. *Journal of Health and Social Behavior*, **21**, 170–80.
15. Stiles, W., Putnam, S., Wolf, M. and James, S. (1979) Interaction exchange structure and patient satisfaction with medical interviews. *Medical Care*, **17**, 667–79.
16. Ley, P. (1982) Satisfaction, compliance and communication. *British Journal of Clinical Psychology*, **21**, 241–54.
17. Linn, L. and Greenfield, S. (1982) Patient suffering and patient satisfaction among the chronically ill. *Medical Care*, **20**, 425–31.
18. Fitzpatrick, R. and Hopkins, A. (1983) Problems in the conceptual framework of patient satisfaction research: an empirical exploration. *Sociology of Health and Illness*, **5**, 297–311.
19. Green, J. (1988) On the receiving end. *Health Services Journal*, 4 Aug, 880–1.
20. Moores, B. and Thompson, A. (1986) An all consuming view. *Health Services Journal*, 3 July, 892–3.
21. Hirschi, T. and Selvin, H. (1973) *Principles of survey analysis*. New York: Free Press.
22. Rossiter, L., Langwell, K., Wan, T. and Rivnyak, M. (1989) Patient satisfaction among elderly enrollees and disenrollees in medicare health maintenance organisations. *Journal of the American Medical Association*, **262**, 57–63.
23. Fitzpatrick, R., Bury, M., Frank, A. and Donnelly, T. (1987) Problems in the assessment of outcome in a back pain clinic. *International Rehabilitation Studies*, **9**, 161–5.

3 | Measurement of impairment, disability and handicap

Shah Ebrahim
Department of Health Care of the Elderly, The London & St Bartholomew's Hospital Medical Colleges, London

The use of mortality data as a measure of the consequences of disease was apparent to John Graunt who in 1662 published a treatise *Natural and political observations upon the Bills of Mortality*. Deaths were linked to living conditions in London, and demonstrated that adverse environments led to more deaths. William Farr, on being made compiler of statistics for the Registrar General in 1838, expanded this system of recording by classifying deaths into three groups: epidemic, sporadic, and external (violent) causes.[1] This simple classification was subsequently developed using a predominantly pathophysiological and anatomical framework, and led to the first International Classification of Disease by the end of the 19th century.

Need for a new taxonomy

The International Classification of Disease (ICD) has been of great use in defining the occurrence of diseases in terms of time, geographical variation and demographic characteristics. The system has been helpful in evaluating the effects of treatment for diseases that commonly result in death, since deaths can be attributed, although sometimes with difficulty, to specific causes. The weakness of classification schemes derived from a disease taxonomy that has its roots in an anatomical, pathological and aetiological framework is apparent when standards of management are worked out for different disease or diagnosis related groups.[2] More severe disease tends to be more expensive to treat, and some index of severity is needed to make adequate comparison of trends.

Clinicians need to measure the severity of disease for many reasons: to decide on treatment, to aid comparisons of management success and failure, to monitor progress, and to estimate prognosis. The new public health, increasingly concerned with the burden of chronic degenerative diseases, with assessing population need for health services, and with making priorities, requires new tools. The ICD lacks the relevant dimensions to group many health problems that cause much suffering (eg visual impairments, immobility, incontinence, cognitive impairment) but which may be caused by many, diverse diseases.

Grouping of such problems can be valuable in identifying a need for new approaches to health care delivery, such as incontinence clinics, memory clinics and so on. Defining disease at levels of the consequences of disease is the fundamental concept behind the International Classification of Impairment, Disability and Handicap (ICIDH).[3]

Definitions

Impairment

Impairment is defined as the anatomical, physiological or biological effects of a disease. This is the level of consequences with which clinicians are most familiar. For example, the impairments caused by asthma are a variable increase in airways resistance, hypertrophy of bronchiolar smooth muscle, and mucous plugging of airways. The attraction of thinking about disease in terms of impairments is that it is often these impairments that are the targets of treatment; they are the means by which severity is usually measured, and they help in monitoring the patient's progress. The very success of the biological approach to disease has tended to blinker clinicians to other possible views.

The growing interest in consumerism in health, together with a better listening ear among doctors, may have contributed to an awareness that treating the biological consequences of disease is not enough. Patients' physiological impairments improved but they failed to feel better; women's breasts were removed to cure the cancer, and fortunately the need to heal the psyche as well was recognised.[4] Patients with myocardial infarction should get better quickly (or die) but some who survived experienced poor results; they did not get back to work and continued to feel ill. Two main hypotheses can be put forward: first, the infarct was more severe than predicted from a solely biological viewpoint; second, some further disease process was at work, such as depression or Dressler's syndrome.

Disability

Disability refers to the impact of disease on the ability to carry out 'tasks' in a manner appropriate to a human being. The range of tasks that can be influenced by a disease is wide (see Table 1). However, the number of tasks or disabilities is much smaller than the number of diseases that

Table 1. The WHO classification of impairments, disabilities and handicaps: a taxonomy of disability

Dimensions of disability

- Locomotion
- Reaching and stretching
- Dexterity
- Seeing
- Hearing

- Personal care
- Continence
- Communication
- Behaviour
- Intellectual function

may lead to immobility, or visual disability for example. This 'common pathway' property of the level of disability consequent on disease is particularly useful for the assessment of the results of treatment of chronic diseases in patients with other, often multiple, pathology. For a single disease, this dimension gives an opportunity to measure the severity of the disease process in a manner that is often highly relevant to the patient, and can be used as a means of monitoring progress. Measures of disability also allow the identification of those patients whose biological or physiological impairment improves, but who remain unable to carry out tasks. Such measures force some thought about the aims and methods of treatment.

Disability measures of self-care are well known, and various scales have been developed since the 1940s to give numerical values to the extent of a disability. Probably the most popular is the Barthel scale,[5] shown in Table 2. The weakness of the Barthel scale is that it is only concerned with self-care, ignoring other aspects of disability. Consequently the top and bottom of the scale do not correspond to the zenith

Table 2. The Barthel 'activities of daily living' (ADL) scale

	With help	Independent
1. Feeding	5	10
2. Moving from wheelchair to bed and return	5–10	15
3. Personal toilet	0	5
4. Getting on and off the toilet	5	10
5. Bathing self	0	5
6. Walking on level surface	10	15
7. Ascending and descending stairs	5	10
8. Dressing	5	10
9. Controlling bowels	5	10
10. Controlling bladder	5	10

A score of zero is given if the patient cannot carry out a task.

and nadir of human ability. The items that make up the scale are arbitrarily weighted; therefore a given score does not correspond to a definable set of disabilities. In practice, its use to monitor therapy is limited by its relative insensitivity to change. However, for some diseases, such as stroke, the magnitude of change in ability may be large, so it performs reasonably well.[6]

Since the World Health Organisation ICIDH was published, much work has gone into producing the questionnaires and severity weightings needed to turn the ICIDH from a taxonomy (ie the pigeon-holes) into an operational tool to measure a person's disabilities. The recent OPCS survey of the prevalence of disability demonstrated that the dimensions of disability described in the ICIDH can be used to describe the burden of disability in the population.[7] It is likely that this system will be more widely adopted by specialists in geriatric medicine and rehabilitation as a means of measuring outcomes.

Handicap

Handicaps are the impact that impairments and disabilities may have on a person's role. People have many different roles: worker, parent, friend etc. There can be a blurring between a disability and a handicap. A mobility disability, say inability to walk outdoors, may lead to a mobility handicap—being stuck indoors all day. Conceptually, it is useful to make the distinction, because the mobility handicap may be alleviated by a friendly neighbour or by arranging attendance at a day centre. The mobility disability and the impairment causing it may be insuperable and lead to a false assumption that 'nothing more can be done'. The difference between disability and handicap underpins the wider goals of the specialties of geriatric medicine and rehabilitation, and also gives insight into the ways in which disabled patients may be helped. Much can be done for such patients provided that the handicaps are identified and possible solutions sought.

Handicaps, because they are defined as roles, are specific to individual patients. A given set of impairments and disabilities will not lead to the same handicaps in every patient. In this way, handicap emphasises the uniqueness of each person, and the need for a unique response. The ICIDH gives a list of survival roles (see Table 3) but does not give a standardised means of putting patients into different handicap pigeon-holes. Philip Wood, the architect of the ICIDH, has said '. . . it is not something ready-made, for use with little further thought . . . it is not a research tool . . . or a system of assessment'.[8] It does not consider other roles in life but is an excellent starting point for trying to make sense of the experience of disease from the patient's view.

Table 3. The WHO classification of impairments, disabilities and handicaps: a taxonomy of handicaps

---

Dimensions of handicap

Survival roles

- Orientation
- Physical independence
- Mobility
- Occupation
- Social integration
- Economic self-sufficiency

Quality of life

It is worth making a brief point about quality of life measurements which are increasingly used as indicators of outcome and need.[9] The starting point for many quality of life scales was the desire to produce an index of health that embodied the WHO definition of health as a state of physical, mental and social well-being—an index that was a positive statement about health, as opposed to a measure related to disease.

In practice, many quality of life scales rely on the presence of symptoms of disease to arrive at a measure of quality of life or well-being. The difficulty of measures of quality of life lies not so much in how the scales are constructed, but more in the conceptual framework within which the scale is used. For example, the Nottingham Health Profile[10] is divided into sub-scales: energy, pain, emotion, social isolation, physical mobility, and sleep. A further set of simple yes/no questions assesses the degree to which health problems interfere with work, social life, hobbies, sex life and so on. The sub-scales measure some symptoms, such as pain and disturbance of sleep, which are related to impairments caused by disease processes. However, other symptoms such as immobility and isolation relate better to disability and handicap. The dimensions of disability and handicap considered by the Nottingham Health Profile, while not arbitrary, represent a narrow range of possible consequences of disease. In general, quality of life scales tend to blur the distinctions between impairment, disability and handicap, measuring a little of each. This in itself is no bad thing, provided that the information is not pooled into an overall score. This can lead to difficulty in using quality of life scores to measure the impact of treatments that may have differential effects on impairment, disability and handicap. The differences between impairments, disabilities and handicaps are too important to lump them together, and doing so muddies the water.

Reasons for making measurements of impairment, disability and handicap (I–D–H)

Measurement can never be divorced from the purpose for which information is sought. The most frequent clinical reasons for measurement of the consequences of disease are to assess the severity of the disease, evaluate success or failure of management, and monitor progress. While these functions are clearly related, the methods of measurement are not necessarily the same.

Severity

Severity is a fundamental concept but, with some exceptions (notably in the fields of head injury, intensive care medicine, neonatology), measures of severity suitable for routine use are poorly developed. The spurs for measuring severity may be the need to compare outcomes for patients managed by different teams, or in different places and times, ie audit. Unless an index of severity is used, unbalanced comparisons may be made. It was clear several years ago that comparisons of perinatal mortality in different parts of the country, and between hospital and general practitioner obstetric units, might be biased.[11] The hospitals had worse perinatal death rates than general practitioner units (and indeed home deliveries), not because management was worse in hospitals but because the severity of the problems dealt with was worse. An adequate comparison had to take into account the differences in the patients treated.

Any unit treating a greater proportion of less severe cases can be made to look better than a unit that gets predominantly the worst cases. For example, on average, a 75-year-old person admitted to a geriatric medical ward will take longer to be discharged than a patient of the same age treated in general medicine.[12] Should the geriatricians be sacked and the general physicians congratulated, or vice versa? An index of severity would allow comparisons of length of stay between patients of comparable ages and severity of illness, thus avoiding a biased assessment of the two styles of service.

The I–D–H scheme is one way to approach measurement of severity of disease. Disease that causes more in the way of impairment, disability and handicap may reasonably be assumed to be worse. It is likely that disease-specific severity measures will be needed as well as more general indicators for elderly patients with multiple pathology. For example, in chronic obstructive airways disease, the whole range of I–D–H may be used as severity measures. The percentage of expected values for various lung function tests, the extent of immobility caused by breathlessness, or the number of days lost from work may all be used to gauge the severity of the condition.

Which index of severity is best? In the past, a tacit assumption has been that the best measure is the one closest to the biological process that is going on; in the case of chronic obstructive airways disease, lung function tests should give the best index of severity. In practice, the best index will be the one that corresponds most closely to prognosis, since this is why we measure severity of disease in the first place. For some diseases a biological measure or measure of impairment will perform best, but for others it will not. The severity of a stroke, for example, when assessed at onset, is best measured by the degree of loss of consciousness over the first 24 hours because it is this that is most closely related to short-term survival.[13] Later on, level of consciousness becomes irrelevant, and aspects of disability such as mobility become a more important determinant of independent survival. The relationships between severity and prognosis are obvious—a good measure of severity will be a good measure of prognosis.

Success and failure: outcome

We need to measure the outcome of treatment, and for many chronic diseases death is simply not a relevant measure. Even for diseases with a high mortality, death and survival may be a relatively inaccurate way of evaluating success and failure.

Randomised controlled clinical trials usually require large numbers of subjects and therefore need to keep measures of outcome simple. Multi-dimensional outcome measures incorporating impairments, disability and handicap caused by a disease are consequently unlikely to be used. The simplest measurement with the smallest variance will produce the most efficient statistical comparison, since small variance leads to small standard errors and increases the power of a study. For example, physiological measurements tend to be precise, and are often used as intermediate outcomes in small trials, when the outcome of real interest, say survival, would require a trial of thousands of subjects.

A Nottingham trial of beta-blockade after acute stroke used this sort of approach.[14] The hypothesis was that beta-blockade would reduce the damage caused by a stroke, and this would be reflected in a reduction in neurological impairments, and a reduction in disability, and in deaths. A natural hierarchy of outcomes was postulated and, since the variance of neurological scores and activities of daily living scores was small, a modest sized trial could be mounted using these measurements as outcomes.[15] A trial using survival as an outcome would require a much larger number of subjects, but could be done if a favourable effect on impairments and disability was found. Indeed, in stroke trials, the measurement of outcome purely in terms of survival will not allow different types of survival (independent, institutional etc) to be compared.

A vital characteristic of an outcome measurement is that it should be sensitive to the degree of change brought about by treatment. Some disability scales, such as the Barthel scale (see Table 2), measure self-care activities in such a crude way that the changes associated with therapy are unlikely to move patients from one category to a less dependent category. Although the scale is sensitive to the spontaneous recovery that occurs after stroke, it is a mistake to equate this sort of sensitivity with the potential effects of treatment, which are likely to be much smaller.

The effects of management may not occur at the level of impairment or disability for many chronic degenerative diseases, where the disease process cannot be halted. Therapists and social workers, and some doctors, may feel that, although they are unable to alter the biological consequences or disability of disease, they are able to improve the patient's quality of life. The handicapping consequences of disease may be reduced by good therapy. At present we are bad at measuring this sort of thing, and much of the audit of rehabilitation is weakened because this essential dimension of handicap is ignored. For example, the Edinburgh Stroke Unit trial demonstrated that, by one year after the stroke, there was no difference in the proportions of patients classed as independent in self-care who had been managed on the stroke unit and on general wards.[16] This may mean that stroke units are a waste of time, but it more probably means that the index of success and failure was too simple and did not reflect the goals of rehabilitation; in short, it failed to discriminate between independence and autonomy. Among stroke

Table 4. An epidemiological appraisal of the outcomes of treatment: the relationship between disability and handicap for a patient treated for an impairment causing a mobility disability

Mobility disability (Unable to walk outdoors)	Mobility handicap (Stuck in one room)	
	Yes	No
Yes	Treatment failure	Major treatment success
No	Can but does not; why?	Treatment success

patients, independence is a good index of how severe the stroke is (reflecting the amount of brain damage), whereas autonomy may give an index of how good rehabilitation has been at coping with the brain damage and disability. An epidemiological perspective, stratifying the two types of outcome, helps to distinguish these differences, as shown in Table 4.

Monitoring progress

I–D–H, because of its wide range, provides a framework for setting rehabilitation goals. Having set goals, part of their achievement rests on monitoring how far away the goal is. It is commonplace for rehabilitation efforts to be spent on patients who have little intrinsic potential.[17] This happens because goals are not clearly defined in I–D–H terms, and progress is assessed subjectively in general statements of 'better', 'ISQ', or 'waiting'.

The potential disabilities and handicaps experienced by patients, and listed in Tables 1 and 3, are a useful *aide memoire* for setting goals, since it is easy to fall into the trap of setting only a limited goal, eg ability to walk indoors, forgetting that to fulfil a survival role a person has to do rather more than walk indoors! Many 'bad discharges' from hospital are a result of the limited medical frame of reference which implies that, provided the patient's impairments have been improved, discharge should not be far away. Patients, families and domiciliary support staff tend to be much more sensitive to the handicapping consequences of disease than we are in hospital. This may be because the hospital so effectively strips patients of anything other than the patient role. Hospital practitioners must guard against losing the ability to picture how a patient will move smoothly from a patient role in hospital to a survival role at home.

Repeatability and validity

Useful I–D–H measurements must possess the characteristics of any measurement: they must be repeatable and they must be valid. Much work has been done on scales of self-care, and the ability to make repeatable measurements is beyond doubt.[18] The repeatability of measurements of handicap is much less well developed, mainly because the production of measurement tools has not taken off in the same way as disability scales. The routine use of disability scales is made difficult because of the multiple sources of information used (different nurses, the patient, the family), and variable definition of the tasks. It is necessary to train staff in their use, and to ensure that standard criteria of passing and failing tasks are defined and used.

Medical thinking about validity is preoccupied with criterion or 'gold standard' validity—the extent to which a measurement compares with the best way of making the measurement. In the case of biological impairments this is appropriate because some superior means of making the measurement is often available. Simple lung function tests may be compared with more elaborate ones, for example. No convenient gold standards exist for tasks or roles; they are done or lived respectively. Social sciences have struggled for a long time with this dilemma of validation of the apparently unvalidatable, and give us alternative concepts of validity: face or content validity, internal consistency, and construct and predictive validities.

The content of a scale can be examined for coverage of the major dimensions of disability to assess face validity. A valid scale will tend to have strong correlations between the component items of the scale and the total score; in other words, it will have high internal consistency. Disability scales can be compared with other disability scales, with length of hospital stay, with final place of discharge, and with survival. These are all examples of construct and predictive validity; provided the disability scale correlates with these other methods of measuring what is happening, then the scale is probably on the right track.

Any 'end user' of an I–D–H measuring tool needs to ask the questions shown in Table 5. This standard format should be used by researchers publishing new measuring techniques.[18] The development of a new measurement is time-consuming and expensive, and should not be undertaken lightly. It is often better to use an off-the-shelf technique that has some limitations than attempt to produce a new method.

Table 5. Questions to ask about an impairment, disability or handicap measurement tool before using it (from Ref. 18)

- Has the method been used with similar patients?
- Is the scope broad enough to cover areas of interest?
- What is the underlying conceptual approach used?
- How feasible (cost, training, time, response rates, acceptability, instruction manual etc) is the method to use?
- How is the method scored, analysed and interpreted?
- Is the method sensitive to the differences or changes expected?
- Is the method only suitable for a screening test (ie false positives and negatives) or is it detailed enough to be used diagnostically?
- How strong and consistent are the data on repeatability and validity of the method?
- How does the method compare with other means of making the measurements?

Interrelationships in the I–D–H model

The model of impairments, disabilities and handicaps suggests a hierarchy, with handicap the worst consequence of disease, and impairment
the least bad. The model also suggests a linear relationship between each
dimension. This is an illusion; in some circumstances an impairment
may be the best measure of severity, and some impairments cause no
overt disability, but are nonetheless handicapping. The best example of
this is of a portwine birthmark which does not interfere with the ability
to carry out any task but may interfere seriously with carrying out roles
in life, such as meeting new people.

It is necessary to understand the relationships between impairments,
disabilities and handicap, because we need to have better measures of
the impact of our work. We need an understanding of the determinants
of disability and handicap equal to our understanding of the determinants of a reduced cardiac output or any other physiological or
biological consequence of disease. We need to have a broad view of the
consequences of disease to enable us to empathise with our patients,
and because we need to use a wide range of treatments to help our
patients overcome the handicapping consequences of disease (even if we
cannot cure the disease process). For example, the measurement of
cardiac output may be sufficient to assess the effects of a new drug.
Cardiac output is a proxy measurement for the biological effects of the
drug on cellular metabolism.

Most clinicians have always realised that treating the disease process
is not the same as treating the whole patient. However, 'treating the
whole patient' is an imprecise way of defining the goals of treatment.
The relationship between improvements in impairments (or biological
effects of disease) and improvements in disability and handicap is not
direct, and it is quite possible for a reduction in impairment to be
associated with no change in disability or handicap. The target of
treatment cannot therefore be placed solely at the biological end of
disease consequences. There is a tendency to invest more importance
(and resources) in making biological measurements, which makes it less
likely that the handicapping consequences of disease will be considered
in as much detail.

An epidemiological study of chronic lung disease illustrates some of
these points.[19] Patients were asked about symptoms of wheeze, whether
dyspnoea made them unable to walk outdoors on the level, and whether
dyspnoea interfered with their normal way of life. Many other questions
were asked, but these three questions reflect impairment (symptom of
wheeze), disability (inability to walk on the level outdoors) and handicap (inability to lead a normal way of life). These three different ways

Table 6. Chronic lung disease in general practice: classification of patients by impairment, disability and handicap, together with lung function tests, GP consultations and use of bronchodilators

	Annual period prevalence	FEV$_1$ predicted	Reversi- bility	Odds of seeing GP	Odds of use of broncho- dilator
Wheeze most days	9.4%	66%	10%	1	1
Wheeze + disability	5.4%	58%	14%	1.7	1.8
Wheeze + handicap	3.7%	58%	17%	6.2	3.2

of expressing the consequences of disease are equally valid, and might be considered to represent a scale of severity. Table 6 shows the percentages of men aged 40–70 years in a general practice who had chronic lung disease expressed in these different ways. The relationship between these three severities of disease and simple lung function tests shows that, while each of the categories was associated with a lower FEV$_1$ than expected, the handicapped patients were no more severely affected than the disabled patients. Perhaps surprisingly, the handicapped patients had a greater airways response to inhaled bronchodilator. Disabled and handicapped patients were much more likely to see their GP and be prescribed bronchodilators than those with frequent wheeze but no disability or handicap.

The I–D–H model of disease consequences applied to chronic lung disease provides a better understanding of several aspects of the disease. The relationship between impairment, disability and handicap follows a logical order, which seems to indicate a dimension of severity since the percentage of sufferers is smaller in each successive category. However, a physiological measure of severity of airflow limitation (FEV$_1$) does not show a clear stepwise gradient from impairment to handicap. The reversibility of the airflow limitation does show a gradient effect, suggesting that handicapped patients may be more treatable. The classification demonstrates quite clearly that disability and handicap are powerful determinants of both patient behaviour (seeing the doctor) and doctor behaviour (prescribing bronchodilators).

As a first approximation, a model of the relationships between impairment, disability and handicap might postulate a linear relationship: for each increment of impairment a corresponding increase in disability occurs. It is then necessary to consider what factors might have some influence on the relationship. For example, ageing might lead to greater disability and handicap per unit of impairment because of reduced homeostatis, weaker muscles and lower cardio-respiratory reserves. A poor home, for example without central heating and with no lift, would further exacerbate the handicapping effects of an impairment. Other factors, such as therapy, aids and appliances, and money, may help to reduce disability and handicap.

Understanding the ways in which impairment, disability and handicap interact may help in developing new approaches to helping patients, and will define more precisely what it is that we do when we practise 'whole person' medicine. It is quite probable that much of the present rehabilitation work done with patients has little or no impact on impairments (eg perceptual re-training, fine hand control), but operates through mechanisms that alleviate handicap.

An expanded I–D–H model

The I–D–H model is a limited framework with which to work when thinking about the consequences of disease. At the level of impairments there will be few problems of measurement provided disease-specific measures are used. Disabilities have been well covered by numerous activities of daily living scales, and more recently other dimensions of disability have been practically applied to measure the prevalence and severity of disability in the population. The dimensions of handicap covered by the WHO classification have not been developed as much, so more resources are needed to produce operational tools to classify handicaps. Many of the quality of life indicators do contain questions that are directly relevant to the measurement of handicap. Such questions could be re-defined as handicap questions rather than added into an overall 'quality of life' score which will tend to hide rather than enhance understanding of the effects of disease or interventions.

In its present form the I–D–H model has a natural appeal to rehabilitation specialists but appears to have contributed little to other areas of medicine. In part this may be due to the upsurge of interest in quality of life measures which have been viewed as outcomes of major importance for many specialists, from oncologists to the pharmaceutical industry.[9] The growth of molecular biology, with its tantalising promises of delivering a fundamental understanding of the basic regulatory mechanisms that go wrong in disease, may have reduced interest in the handicap end of the spectrum. Neither a biological nor a handicap view of the effects of disease is sufficient for all purposes; they are complementary ways of looking at the same problem. Table 7 shows an expanded I–D–H model[20] which breaks the impairment category into biological and anatomical/physiological levels. This is the territory of clinical scientists, and is a relevant level of measuring outcome (or severity) for

Table 7.   An expanded impairment–disability–handicap (I–D–H) model

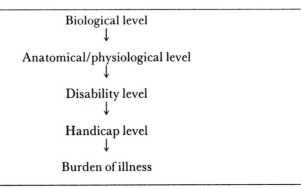

many diseases. The next levels are of disability and handicap which must be distinguished from each other. A final level of 'burden of illness' is needed to encompass the wider concerns of population science, and to acknowledge that health services have goals that can best be measured in terms of a reduction in the burden of illness.

This expanded I–D–H model demonstrates that the frames of reference that separate scientists and therapists, both clinically and ideologically, can be fitted into a single model of the consequences of disease. The next step is to ensure that this model is used for describing the consequences of disease in trials to evaluate the effects of new treatments, when auditing care, for monitoring progress, and for the assessment of need.

References

1. Langmuir, A.D. (1976) William Farr: founder of modern concepts of surveillance. *International Journal of Epidemiology*, **5**, 13–8.
2. Omenn, G.S. and Conrad, D.A. (1984) Implications of DRGs for clinicians. *New England Journal of Medicine*, **311**, 1314–7.
3. World Health Organisation (1980) *International classification of impairments, disabilities and handicaps.* Geneva: WHO.
4. Dean, C. (1988) The emotional impact of mastectomy. *British Journal of Hospital Medicine*, **39**, 30–9.
5. Mahoney, F.I. and Barthel, D.W. (1965) Functional evaluation: the Barthel index. *Maryland State Medical Journal*, **14**, 61–5.
6. Wade, D.T. and Collin, C. (1988) The Barthel ADL index: a standard measure of physical disability. *International Disability Studies*, **10**, 64–7.
7. Martin, J., Meltzer, H. and Eliot, D. (1988) *The prevalence of disability among adults.* OPCS surveys of disability in Great Britain, Report 1. London: HMSO.
8. Wood, P.H.N. (1987) Maladies imaginaires: some common misconceptions about the ICIDH. *International Disability Studies*, **9**, 125–8.
9. Walker, S.R. and Rosser, R.M. (eds) (1988) *Quality of life: assessment and application.* Lancaster: MTP Press.

10. Hunt, S.M., McEwen, J. and McKenna, S.P. (1986) *Measuring health status.* London: Croom Helm.
11. Alberman, E. (1980) Prospects for better perinatal health. In *Better perinatal health.* London: The Lancet.
12. Rai, G.S., Murphy, P. and Pluck, R.A. (1985) Who should provide hospital care of elderly people. *Lancet,* **i,** 683–5.
13. Barer, D.H. and Mitchell, J.R.A. (1989) Predicting the outcome of acute stroke: do multivariate methods help? *Quarterly Journal of Medicine,* **261,** 27–39.
14. Barer, D.H., Cruickshank, J.M., Ebrahim, S. and Mitchell, J.R.A. (1988) Low dose beta-blockade in acute stroke (BEST trial): an evaluation. *British Medical Journal,* **296,** 737–41.
15. Barer, D.H., Ebrahim, S. and Mitchell, J.R.A. (1988) The pragmatic approach to stroke trial design: stroke register, pilot trial, assessment of neurological and then functional outcome. *Neuroepidemiology,* **7,** 1–12.
16. Garraway, W.M., Akhtar, A.J., Hockey, L. and Prescott, R.J. (1980) Management of acute stroke in the elderly: follow-up of a controlled trial. *British Medical Journal,* **281,** 827–9.
17. Brocklehurst, J.C., Andrews, K., Richards, B. and Laycock, P.J. (1978) How much physical therapy for patients with stroke? *British Medical Journal,* **1,** 1307–10.
18. McDowell, I. and Newell, C. (1987) *Measuring health: a guide to rating scales and questionnaires.* Oxford: Oxford University Press.
19. Littlejohns, P., Ebrahim, S. and Anderson, H.R. (1989) Prevalence and diagnosis of chronic respiratory symptoms in adults. *British Medical Journal,* **298,** 1556–60.
20. Stein, R.E.K., Gortmaker, S.L., Perrin, E.C. *et al.* (1987) Severity of illness: concepts and measurements. *Lancet,* **ii,** 1506–9.

4 | Assessment of pain, and effectiveness of treatment

H.J. McQuay
Oxford Regional Pain Relief Unit, Abingdon Hospital, Oxfordshire

'Accurate appraisal of the biochemical, neuronal and psychological mechanisms of pain depends heavily on the assessment of pain in human subjects. Man's unique verbal abilities open a window to private experience, and only through such experience is pain defined.'[1]

At the moment there is no way to measure someone's pain reliably by sampling blood or urine or, for example, by measuring changes in temperature or in the electroencephalogram. In the absence of such objective methods, measurement of pain amounts to recording the patient's report of his pain. Such subjective measures are often disparaged, but measurement of pain can be remarkably sensitive and reproducible, provided that the measurements are done properly. They have been used successfully to measure and to compare the efficacy of new and established treatments, both for pharmacological and for other types of intervention. However, the refinement of methods has occurred primarily in the context of acute interventions; the chronic setting has not received the same degree of attention. The methods have been refined and used to measure relative change after an intervention rather than to determine the absolute state of pain. Another problem is that by their very nature the methods require communication between the patient and the observer. There are clinical contexts in which this may not be possible, for example in very young children and in any patient who is incapable of reliable communication. Those who are unconscious or terminally ill may present particular problems. This paper will discuss the methods available and their clinical and research shortcomings. Very little work has been done on outcome in this field. Some approaches are suggested.

Rating pain

Scales

Patients' reports of pain intensity and relief are usually determined by using binary, categorical or visual analogue scales. Binary scales are

Table 1. Categorical verbal rating scales

Pain intensity		Pain relief	
Severe	3	Complete	4
Moderate	2	Good	3
Slight	1	Moderate	2
None	0	Slight	1
		None	0

designed to elicit a yes/no answer to a question such as: Is your pain more than half relieved? The commonest categorical scales use words, and the patient is asked to choose the word that is most appropriate. Examples of such scales are shown in Table 1.

Visual analogue scales are usually presented as 10-cm horizontal lines. The versions that we use, with their end markers, are shown in Fig. 1.

Binary scales are simple, and questions such as — "Is more than half your pain relieved?" — clinically relevant. Optimal sensitivity for the other scales is often achieved by operating at a low point on the dose response curve, a point at which few patients would have more than half their pain relieved. Binary scales are unfashionable. The verbal categorical scales are simple and universal, but impose particular categories on the patient. Visual analogue scales are more complex, and hence less universal. The reported major limitations to their use are in the elderly and in patients who are sleepy. There is a considerable literature on the results obtained with visual analogue scales concerning the influence of the orientation of the line, intermediate markings, presence or absence of line labels and previous line presentations. Using the lines shown in

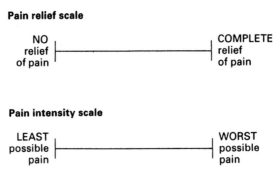

Fig. 1. *Visual analogue scales for pain relief and pain intensity.*

Fig. 1, we have found that previous presentations (as when patients complete diaries with visual analogues) do not preclude obtaining sensible results, given adequate explanation. The clinical utility of nursing pain charts, the analogue lines of which break most of the purist rules about intermediate markings and orientation, also suggests that these rules are not crucial.

Relief of pain vs intensity of pain

When the need is to measure the state of pain rather than the effect of an intervention, pain intensity rather than relief scales are appropriate. In contexts where both relief and intensity scales are appropriate, the question arises as to which is 'best'. Pain relief scales measure something slightly different from pain intensity. Relief may be more of a composite dimension for the patient than intensity, because any side effects of the intervention, such as nausea, may be included in this judgement. Relief also requires memory, because the patient has to judge what the pain was like before and balance that against what the pain is like now in order to gauge the relief. It is often suggested that this makes relief scales more complex than intensity scales and perhaps less useful. This has not been our experience. Over a considerable number of studies using multiple relief and intensity scales, the relief scales (analogue or categorical) have proved to be more sensitive. In diary studies, relief scales may be sensitive to patients' activity which will not be the case for intensity scales.

Categorical and visual analogue scales

Considerable work comparing categorical and visual analogue scales used simultaneously in different settings has shown that the two methods correlate well, so they are measuring the same thing, be it intensity or relief. The evidence is conflicting as to which is more sensitive and/or reproducible. Within our own studies, sometimes visual analogue and sometimes categorical scales prove more sensitive, and there is no clear advantage within acute and chronic pain contexts or even within observations made by a particular nurse observer. Our general rule is that when simplicity is the most important factor, as might be the case for outpatient diary work, then our choice would be categorical scales.

Single or multiple scales

When precision is all-important then we use multiple scales at each sample point. The reason is not that the scales are independent, that is that each is a measure of something different, but because, if the patient provides measurements on one or more of the scales which are clearly incompatible with the readings on other scale(s), then the nurse observer has the opportunity to re-question at this sample time. In contexts where there is no nurse observer present when the patient makes the measurements, such as in outpatient diary studies, then disparities between measurements made at the same sample time on different scales allow one to decide how to weight the measurements. Multiple scales can thus reduce the noise in the measurements.

Questionnaires

One obvious criticism of the rating scales is that they concentrate on one dimension only, ie intensity or relief of the sensation of pain, ignoring the quality of the pain. An analogy is to describe the brightness of a visual stimulus and ignore the colour.

One method of pain measurement which gets around this problem is the McGill Pain Questionnaire (MPQ).[2] The 78 adjectives in 20 groups in the questionnaire are arranged to reflect three dimensions of pain: sensory, affective and evaluative. This questionnaire can yield three indices of pain: a pain rating index based on the scale values of the words chosen by the patient; a rank score using the rank values within each subgroup chosen; and lastly the total number of adjectives chosen by the patient. The sensitivity and reproducibility of the MPQ have been well established. It has been widely used in studies on chronic pain, both as a measure of state of pain and to follow the effects of interventions. It has been used to a lesser extent in studies on acute pain. This is in part due to the greater time which the MPQ requires at each sample time compared with categorical or visual analogue scales, and in part to the fact that the visual analogue scales work effectively in most acute pain states. The issue of the quality of the pain, which the MPQ can detect and the other scales do not, is more important in chronic pain. In following patients with pain due to cancer whose pain is associated with lymphoedema, the MPQ has proved considerably more sensitive than categorical or analogue scales.[3]

Charting pain

There is a clinical need to be able to record the state of patients' pain, both intermittently at outpatient visits or serially as an inpatient or at home. A number of charts and methods have been proposed. The features include:

Analogue or categorical assessment of intensity or relief of pain
A picture of the body so that site of pain may be recorded

Space to record measures used to combat pain
Unwanted effects of treatment

Our current version is shown in Fig. 2. We have reverted to categorical scales for simplicity as we usually use this chart for outpatients. There is no body picture because the majority of the patients have pain at only one site. In clinical contexts in which patients have multiple sites of pain, this may be inadequate. The chart from the Burford Nursing Development Unit (Fig. 3)[4] includes a section in which the names of drugs and dosage can be included. This is excluded on our chart because we already know the drugs and dosage used. These charts are undoubtedly an advance in the service setting. They were not designed for precise studies. This is reflected in the lack of relief scales and use of intermediate markings on the analogue scale.

These charts have particular value in indicating to medical staff who are not with the patient continuously just how good is the management of the patient's pain. It is less useful if the chart is instituted after the patient's pain has become a significant problem. We have found it best, in the appropriate contexts, to make charts part of the routine of nursing care, analogous to charts of blood pressure and temperature. In that way they are filled in, and a 'previous pain history' is available if problems arise.

Drug consumption

A simple but relatively crude method of measuring the efficacy of an intervention is to record to what extent (if any) the intervention reduces the need for other analgesics or, in the case of an intervention with short duration of effect, how long it is before the patient requires further analgesia.

Use of such 'time to next analgesic' (TNA) measurements has proved useful in contexts in which nurse observer methodology is not available, or the effect of the intervention is too prolonged for constant attendance by a nurse observer. We have used it effectively both with spinal opiates, which have a long duration of effect,[5] and also to show the effects of premedication and local anaesthetic blocks on post-operative pain.[6] TNA measurements are, however, subject to the bias of formal drug-rounds, at which drugs are dispensed by the nurses. The interval between these rounds may define the sensitivity of the measurement.

A method by which the relief of pain is estimated from the consumption of a drug is the use of patient-controlled analgesia (PCA). If the intervention has a long duration of effect, such as 10 or even 24 hours, the nurse observer method may be inappropriate owing to the long study

Oxford Pain Chart

Name ....

Treatment Week ....

Please fill in this chart each evening before going to bed. Record your pain intensity and the amount of pain relief. If you have had any side-effects please note them in the side-effects box.

Date									
Pain Intensity — How bad has your pain been today?	severe								
	moderate								
	mild								
	none								
Pain Relief — How much pain relief have the tablets given today?	complete								
	good								
	moderate								
	slight								
	none								
Side effects — Has the treatment upset you in any way?									

How effective was the treatment this week? *poor fair good very good excellent* Please circle your choice.

Fig. 2. *Oxford pain chart.*

PAIN CHART

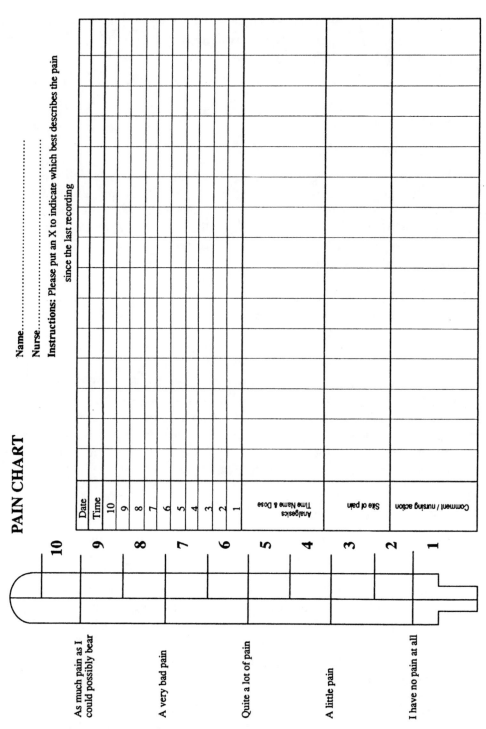

Fig. 3. *Modified Burford pain chart.*[4]

period. If a finer tool than the relatively crude TNA is required, PCA is a real alternative. It has not yet been validated against the nurse observer method but is likely to prove very useful.[7,8]

Trial design

Number and composition of trial groups

It is important that trial design should include an index of sensitivity, an indication that the methods used are capable of distinguishing an effective from an ineffective intervention. Perhaps the commonest pitfall is to compare one dose of the test drug with one dose of a standard drug. If clear separation in effect is found, the result can be interpreted. However, if the two medications produce superimposable time–effect curves, the result may be very difficult to interpret. An index of sensitivity is advisable. This is achieved in the classical single-dose design by showing separation of efficacy between negative control (placebo) and a standard analgesic. The positive control design alternative uses separation of two doses (low and high) of the standard as the index of sensitivity.

Both positive and negative control designs come close to fulfilling both explanatory and pragmatic[9] intentions in the same study, by simultaneously answering the explanatory question as to whether or not the test intervention has greater efficacy than placebo (or low dose of standard) and fulfilling the pragmatic role by comparing the test intervention with existing standard clinical regimes.

Parallel group or crossover

Crossover designs mean that 40% fewer patients are needed than in other designs.[10] A criticism of crossover studies is that the baseline pain may change for the different treatments, decreasing with time postoperatively, or varying with time in many chronic pain conditions. The initial intensity of pain for the various treatment periods may therefore be different. Because the methodology uses relative change from initial pain for each treatment this is not an insuperable criticism. We have used crossover designs postoperatively to good effect, showing the additional analgesic benefit of 20 mg codeine base with 400 mg ibuprofen.[11] The major practical limitation to crossover designs is logistic. Patients spend less and less time in hospital, and running crossover trials of postoperative analgesia particularly is becoming increasingly difficult as a result. In patients with pain due to cancer, it may be very difficult to run crossovers for an extended period owing to deteriorating clinical condition.

Which drug to use as standard comparator?

The standard opiate for clinical use is morphine, and morphine is used as the comparator for most opiate studies. Problems arise with choice of comparator when drugs from different classes are being compared, such as opiate and non-steroidal anti-inflammatory drugs (NSAIDs). The two classes of drug may produce completely distinct unwanted effects, so the choice of standard drug may affect the blinding of the study. Studies comparing parenteral opiate with oral NSAID are particularly at risk. Comparing drugs across routes (eg sublingual opiate and oral NSAID) may also create problems, requiring a double-dummy technique.

In some chronic pain syndromes (see below) the pain may be relatively or absolutely insensitive to conventional analgesics. The choice of such drugs as standards for patients with such pain means that no sensitivity can be shown. False negative results may be produced by such a study.

The rules

Categorical and analogue scales have been used successfully many times to show the effects of analgesics in single dosage. The example shown in Fig. 4 is typical. From such data, slopes can be derived for the determina-

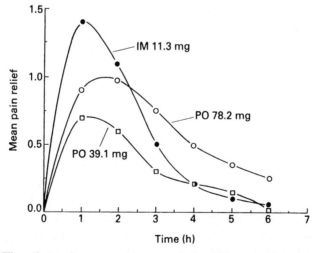

Fig. 4   *The relation between mean pain relief and interval since administration of oral morphine (39.1 and 78.2 mg) and of intramuscular morphine (11.3 mg). Redrawn from Ref. 12.*

tion of potency ratios. Derived from crossover studies in postoperative pain, the commonest model until recently because of convenience, the data have stood the test of time. Successful use of the classic method does, however, require that certain rules are not broken.[12,13]

The rules include double-blind medication, ensuring that observations on any patient are made by the same observer, and a study design with either negative control (placebo) or positive control (two doses of standard drug). In addition, to ensure sensitivity there must be a sufficient degree of pain that any decrease can be measured; the intensity of pain before the intervention should be the equivalent of moderate or severe on the categorical verbal intensity of pain scale (Table 1). Giving analgesics to patients whose intensity of pain is none or mild means that there may be insufficient pain for the intervention to show any measurable effect.

These guidelines are applicable to studies of subjective response in fields other than analgesia. Experimental design must compensate for the non-specific influences such as patient–observer interaction, prejudice from prior information, and the error and variability arising within and between patients. Two examples from analgesic studies in postoperative oral surgery show the effect of a methodological flaw due to breaking the criterion that the initial pain should be moderate or severe. Both studies used elapsed time after surgery rather than intensity of pain as the criterion for giving the test analgesic, and resulted in the findings (erroneous in my judgement) that dihydrocodeine was not an analgesic in pain after oral surgery[14] and that the dose response to intravenous morphine was quantal rather than graded.[15]

Other than errors due to poor methodology mentioned above, the first source of confusion which may arise with this 'classic' method is when the comparison involves drugs (or the same drug) given by different routes. There may be a difference in the rate of absorption of the formulations. The oral to parenteral ratio for peak analgesic effect of morphine was determined as 1 : 6 in such a single-dose crossover study.[12] The disparity between this result and the ratio of 1 : 2 or 1 : 3 used commonly in palliative care when changing from parenteral to oral formulations has resulted in much continuing controversy.[16] It is, however, explicable on the basis that the single-dose study downgrades the efficacy of the oral dose because of slow absorption compared with the intramuscular dose over the 6-hour study period, and because the clinical yardstick in palliative care is related more to total relief than to peak effect. The disparity highlights the fact that there are surprisingly few studies of the effects of multiple doses of analgesic. Such studies are necessary to answer clinically important issues.

Another example of confusion associated with the route of administration occurs with spinal opiates. Intrathecal and extradural administration of opiates can produce extended duration of analgesia compared with conventional routes. The classic method of measuring analgesia (nurse observer collection of subjective response data) is logistically difficult if the analgesic under test is effective for much longer than 6 hours; the 12 (extradural) or 24 hours (intrathecal) duration of the spinal opiates highlight this problem. Cruder measures, such as the time to next analgesic or subsequent analgesic consumption, have however been sufficiently sensitive to show a relationship between dosage and response by these novel routes. Patient-controlled analgesia has also proved effective.

A second source of confusion is due to the ceiling to efficacy. Partial agonists and mixed agonist–antagonists have in general not shown the ceiling to analgesic effect expected from their pharmacology,[17] presumably because the ceiling is not reached within the normal therapeutic range. An exception is nalbuphine. Potency ratios were quite different in a variety of clinical contexts, and the ceiling was exposed as the severity of the pain increased. Laboratory pharmacology also predicts that testing for the efficacy of a partial agonist or mixed agonist–antagonist together with or following the use of agonist will necessarily alter the dose–response curve. This is of great importance clinically (and for efficacy studies), particularly because of sequential agonist/mixed agonist–antagonist use postoperatively and vice versa in chronic cancer pain, but within the normal clinical dose range there is little evidence for such dose–response curve shift;[18,19] the important caveat is that prior narcotic exposure can indeed produce such shifts.[19]

A ceiling to efficacy is also seen with NSAIDs, higher doses failing to produce proportionate increases in analgesia as measured by peak or total analgesic effect in single-dose studies. Such proportional increase in efficacy may be apparent if duration of effect is determined rather than peak effect. Survival analysis is one way by which this may be achieved. The explanation for the flat curves for peak effect may lie in the very real analgesic potency of these drugs, which have proved indistinguishable in oral formulation from parenteral opiates in a variety of clinical pains. An asymptote may be reached on the dose–response curve if the doses given are more than adequate for the pain stimulus studied.

Multiple dosing studies

There is no special reason why these methods should not be applied to multiple dosing studies. The reason that there are fewer such studies is logistic; they are demanding of time and effort. Outpatient studies are feasible, using either assessments at clinic visits or diaries completed by the patients,[20-22] and success in inpatient studies can also be achieved.[23] We have found compliance to be good, perhaps because patients in pain remember to take their medication.

Applying the methodology in chronic pain

The problems that arise when applying these methods in chronic pain are due to the special nature of some of the pain syndromes. Implicit in applying the classic method to acute pain is the idea that the standard analgesic in the design will have guaranteed efficacy. In some chronic pain syndromes this assumption may not be valid.

The crucial distinction is the nature of the pain. Drugs effective as sole analgesics in acute pain have proved effective in chronic *nociceptive* pain, and this is valid for the range of conventional analgesics from aspirin through to morphine. In *deafferentation* pain, however, this is not the case.[24,25]

There is thus a need to define the pain context. One example is that the failure to demonstrate analgesic dose response for antidepressants as sole analgesics in acute pain was not predictive of co-analgesic efficacy,[26] and it was not predictive for prolonged deafferentation pain, where antidepressants were effective as the sole analgesic.[27] A negative result in acute pain as sole analgesic is therefore a likely predictor of lack of efficacy in prolonged nociceptive pain, but not for prolonged de-afferentation pain.

What this means for studies in chronic pain is that, if analgesics for nociceptive pain are to be studied, the character of the pain (nociceptive or deafferentation) must be a criterion for entry to the study. False negative results would result for such drugs if studied in patients with deafferentation type pain.

The heterogeneity of the conditions associated with deafferentation pain means that group designs may not be the most practicable. If there are differences in the sensitivity of the pain to particular classes of drugs, such differential sensitivity means that group designs may be inappropriate because a proportion of the patients in a group may have no sensitivity to the active drugs (test or standard) under treatment. What drug should be used as the standard for deafferentation pain? This is a very difficult question to answer except on an individual patient basis. This is where the clinical need and opportunity for studies using single-patient trial designs arises. The single-patient or n of 1 design[28] seeks the effective treatment for that particular patient. In the multiple dose crossover the effective treatment for the group is sought. The more subtle difference between the two approaches is that the definition of sensitivity is possible *within* the n of 1 design, whereas if group designs are really considered necessary the sensitivity of the patients to the drug class under test should be established before embarking on the multiple dose crossover. Clinically relevant examples of the *n* of 1 design in contexts other than pain include dyspnoea[29] and metronidazole in ileostomy inflammation.[30]

The clinical requirements suggested for such *n* of 1 designs include reversible action, rapid onset of effect and rapid termination of effect.[28] The extent to which these are relative rather than absolute requirements is unclear but may be critical for application of these designs to research work on pain. Two drug classes for which we particularly need good controlled data and for which the single-patient designs may be of great help are the antidepressants and anticonvulsants, which are used widely to treat pain described as burning or shooting.

Effectiveness of treatment

The effectiveness of pain management has been sadly neglected. In most circumstances in acute pain there is no excuse for ineffective care; that such ineffective care is a common experience is an indictment of our ability or motivation to deliver what is necessary when it is needed. Widespread use of the simple pain charts mentioned above could act as an assessment of the quality of delivery of pain relief; we know it will work if properly delivered. The risk/benefit ratio for invasive methods of relieving pain has still to be compared with that for simpler methods delivered on time.

The effectiveness of treatment for many patients with chronic cancer pain has been greatly improved by the use of procedures emanating from the hospice movement. These procedures recommend a staged titration of drugs, initially non-opiates then opiates if necessary, titrating dose

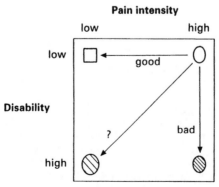

Fig. 5. *Effectiveness of treatment judged on the axes of pain intensity and disability.*

against pain. An important simplification is the use of a limited number of drugs with which the prescriber is familiar.

Measures of effectiveness of pain relief are badly needed for chronic pain conditions (both non-malignant and malignant) for which there is no single effective treatment. Relative efficacy needs to be compared on the dual axes of distress and disability (Fig. 5). Within one condition, such as trigeminal neuralgia, the choice of treatments includes carbamazepine, neurosurgery, freezing the relevant division of the trigeminal nerve (cryoprobe) or burning the nerve (radiofrequency). Each of these procedures may reduce pain intensity (distress). Each also produces some disability. A third axis, recurrence of the pain, may also be relevant in judging overall effectiveness. The technical efficacy of the procedures, the stage in the disease history at which they are performed and the order in which they are performed may well influence outcome. Without information we cannot make sensible choices.

References

1. Gracely, R.H. (1980) Pain measurement in man. In *Pain, discomfort and humanitarian care* (ed. J.J. Bonica) p 111. Amsterdam: Elsevier/North Holland.
2. Melzack, R. (1975) The McGill pain questionnaire: major properties and scoring methods. *Pain*, **1**, 277–99.
3. Carroll, D., Badger, C., McQuay, H.J. and Twycross, R.G. (1988) Pain and lymphoedema. *Journal of Pain and Symptom Management*, **3**, S24.
4. Burford Nursing Development Unit (1984) Nurses and pain. *Nursing Times*, **18**, 94.
5. Moore, R.A., Paterson, G.M.C., Bullingham, R.E.S. *et al.* (1984) A controlled comparison of intrathecal cinchocaine with intrathecal cinchocaine and morphine; plasma morphine concentrations and clinical effects. *British Journal of Anaesthesia*, **56**, 837–41.
6. McQuay, H.J., Carroll, D. and Moore, R.A. (1988) Postoperative orthopaedic pain: the effect of opiate premedication and local anaesthetic blocks. *Pain*, **33**, 291–5.
7. McQuay, H.J., Bullingham, R.E.S., Evans, P.J.D. *et al.* (1980) Demand analgesia to assess pain relief from epidural opiates. *Lancet*, **i**, 768–9.
8. Watson, P.J.Q., McQuay, H.J., Bullingham, R.E.S. *et al.* (1982) Single-dose comparison of buprenorphine 0.3 and 0.6 mg iv given after operation: clinical effects and plasma concentrations. *British Journal of Anaesthesia*, **54**, 37–43.
9. Schwartz, D. and Lellouch, J. (1967) Explanatory and pragmatic attitudes in therapeutic trials. *Journal of Chronic Disease*, **20**, 637–48.
10. James, K.E., Forrest, W.H. and Rose, R.L. (1985) Crossover and noncrossover designs in four-point line analgesic assays. *Clinical Pharmacology and Therapeutics*, **37**, 242–52.
11. McQuay, H.J., Carroll, D., Watts, P.G. *et al.* (1989) Codeine 20 mg increases pain relief from ibuprofen 400 mg after third molar surgery. *Pain*, **40**, 1–2.
12. Houde, R.W., Wallenstein, S.L. and Beaver, W.T. (1965) Clinical measurement of pain. In *Analgetics* (ed. G.D. Stevens) pp 75–122. New York and London: Academic Press.
13. Lasagna, L. (1980) Analgesic methodology: a brief history and commentary. *Journal of Clinical Pharmacology*, **20**, 273–6.

14. Seymour, R.A., Rawlins, M.D. and Rowell, F.J. (1982) Dihydrocodeine-induced hyperalgesia in postoperative dental pain. *Lancet*, **i**, 1425–6.
15. Levine, J.D., Gordon, N.C., Smith, R. and Fields, H.L. (1981) Analgesic responses to morphine and placebo in individuals with post-operative pain. *Pain*, **14**, 379–88.
16. Kaiko, R.F. (1986) Commentary: equianalgesic dose ratio of intramuscular/oral morphine, 1 : 6 versus 1 : 3. In *Opioid analgesics in the management of cancer pain* (ed. K. Foley and C. Inturrisi) [*Advances in pain research and therapy*, Vol. 8] pp 87–93. New York: Raven Press.
17. Bullingham, R.E.S., McQuay, H.J. and Moore, R.A. (1983) Clinical pharmacokinetics of narcotic agonist/antagonist drugs. *Clinical Pharmacokinetics*, **8**, 332–43.
18. Levine, J.D. and Gordon, N.C. (1988) Synergism between the analgesic actions of morphine and pentazocine. *Pain*, **33**, 369–72.
19. Houde, R.W., Wallenstein, S.L. and Rogers, A. (1972) Interactions of pentazocine and morphine (Analgesic studies program of the Sloan-Kettering Institute for Cancer Research). In *Report of the 34th Annual Scientific Meeting of the Committee on Problems of Drug Dependence*, pp 153–64. National Academy of Sciences.
20. Watson, C.P.N. and Evans, R.J. (1985) A comparative trial of amitriptyline in post-herpetic neuralgia. *Pain*, **23**, 387–94.
21. McQuay, H., Carroll, D., Moxon, A. *et al.* (1990) Benzydamine cream for the treatment of postherpetic neuralgia: minimum duration of treatment periods in a crossover trial. *Pain*, in press.
22. Max, M.B., Schafer, S.C., Culnane, M. *et al.* (1988) Amitriptyline, but not lorazepam, relieves postherpetic neuralgia. *Neurology*, **38**, 1427–32.
23. Stambaugh, J.E. and McAdams, J. (1987) Comparison of intramuscular dezocine with butorphanol and placebo in chronic cancer pain: a method to evaluate analgesia after both single and repeated doses. *Clinical Pharmacology and Therapeutics*, **42**, 210–9.
24. Arner, S. and Meyerson, B.A. (1988) Lack of analgesic effect of opioids on neuropathic and idiopathic forms of pain. *Pain*, **33**, 11–23.
25. McQuay, H.J. (1988) Pharmacological treatment of neuralgic and neuropathic pain. *Cancer Surveys*, **7**, 141–59.
26. Levine, J.D., Gordon, N.C., Smith, R. and McBryde, R. (1986) Desipramine enhances opiate postoperative analgesia. *Pain*, **27**, 45–9.
27. Watson, C.P., Evans, R.J., Reed, K. *et al.* (1982) Amitriptyline versus placebo in post-herpetic neuralgia. *Neurology*, **54**, 37–43.
28. Editorial (1986) Single-patient trials. *Lancet*, **i**, 1254–5.
29. Guyatt, G., Sackett, D., Taylor, W.D. *et al.* (1986) Determining optimal therapy: randomised trials in individual patients. *New England Journal of Medicine*, **314**, 889–92.
30. McLeod, R.S., Taylor, D.W., Cohen, Z. and Cullen, J.B. (1986) Single-patient randomised clinical trial. *Lancet*, **i**, 726–8.

5 | Relationship between appropriateness and outcome

Robert H. Brook

Departments of Medicine and Public Health, UCLA Center for the Health Sciences, and The RAND Corporation, Santa Monica, California, USA

Why would anyone wish to write a paper on the relationship between the appropriateness and outcome of care? Is it not obvious that care that is more appropriate would lead to better outcome, ie improved health? If this is not so, then exploring the reasons for this lack of correlation requires us to begin at the beginning, namely, to define the terms quality of care, appropriateness and outcome. Quality of care causes the health of a patient or a community to deviate for the better from its natural course in accordance with the patient's or the community's desires.[1] The focus of quality of care is on those services delivered in the personal health care system, and when quality is high the personal care system produces the maximum deviation towards better health. In order to deliver high quality of care, or to determine whether it exists, a practitioner or researcher must decide the following:

1. What is the population for whom he is responsible? Those who visit him? Those on a list? Those employed by a business? Those residing in a geographic area?

2. What are the health desires or wishes of the 'enrolled' population? If a patient has a disease for which there are a variety of acceptable treatments that result in different health consequences, delivering high quality care requires assessing potential trade-offs and health preferences. Trade-offs are of at least two types—between delayed versus immediate health benefits and between different types of health (physical and mental). For example, two acceptable therapies are available for squamous cell lung cancer—surgery and irradiation. It is probably the case that the 5 years survival for patients treated by surgery is greater than for those patients treated by radiation therapy. However, surgery is associated with a non-trivial possibility of immediate death. This produces a trade-off between the possibility of immediate death and the likelihood, if one survives surgery, of a

longer life expectancy. Deciding which therapeutic option represents high quality care is dependent upon assessing, at least, a patient's risk-taking attitude, age and the quality of the care actually delivered. McNeil and her co-workers found that, when 60-year-old patients were asked which therapy they preferred, 7% would choose radiation therapy (ie give up some long-term benefit for no immediate risk of death) if the surgical death rate was 5%. However, the number rose to 64% if the operative death rate was 20%.[2]

3. What procedures or tests or drugs should be used, and in what combination or order?

4. Who should do the procedure and in what circumstances?

In answering the above four questions, a patient would most likely wish to undergo those procedures that improve his conceptualisation of health; this means that the positive health consequences of having the procedure would, on average, exceed the negative health risks of the procedure. Health benefits and risks would include, among others, longevity, physical and mental functioning, pain, worry, anxiety produced by a false positive result, and labelling. The patient would not want to have either too few or too many procedures performed on him. In addition, he would want to make sure that the procedures were performed in a manner that produced the best possible result. He would like to go to the practitioner who set the outcome standard in the field, ie had the 1% post-operative death rate as opposed to the 10% death rate. Finally, the patient would expect that the doctor or health system must accomplish all of the above in a manner that is consistent with human values, dignity and ethical behaviour.

In order to define correctly appropriateness and outcome of care, and to discover the relationship between them, one must relate definitions of them to the attributes of quality previously described. To judge or measure the appropriateness of, for example, the use of coronary artery bypass surgery, one must first define, in clinical terms, the population to whom the appropriateness standards or guidelines will apply. In the case of bypass surgery, this might be men with severe angina (Canadian heart classification III or IV) whose pain is unresponsive to medical therapy and who have left main disease on coronary angiography.[3]

Next, one must select a method by which standards or guidelines to judge appropriateness could be developed. First, agreement must be reached on a definition of appropriateness. Such a definition might be implicit and represent the global opinion of a single physician or a group of physicians. It might be explicit and define appropriateness as a trade-off between health benefits and health risks when the average person with the specified clinical characteristics went to the average practitioner.

It might relate to these health trade-offs when care was given by the best practitioner instead of the average one,[4] or it might include costs to the patient or to society in the definition of appropriateness. After a definition is agreed upon, information must be marshalled to help develop the standard. The information would come from the literature and include data from controlled trials, observational studies and case reports, but it could also include the clinical opinion of physicians. The mechanism for synthesising the information could be based on a number of techniques and take advantage of a science court, committee meetings or the delphi technique. The rating of appropriateness could be global and be based, after a review of the literature, on answering a question such as, on a 1 to 9 scale: How appropriate in a specific clinical circumstance is the procedure?[5] The judgement process could be disaggregated into estimates of probabilities of specific outcomes that could be obtained with or without the procedure, and estimates of patient utilities associated with those outcomes.

For example, the method we used to determine the appropriateness of the use of carotid endarterectomy had the following components:[6]

1. A literature review was performed which identified studies that examined the efficacy and effectiveness of carotid endarterectomy, its use, what people said about how it should or should not be used, and whether those recommendations were based on results of randomised controlled clinical trials or other types of clinical studies.

2. After reading the literature review, local experts were asked to help identify homogeneous clinical populations or indications to whom carotid endarterectomy could or could not be applied. The indications covered all potential uses of the procedure and 864 clinically homogeneous populations were identified. For example, one group consisted of patients who had one carotid transient ischaemic attack in the past year, had never received medical therapy, were at low surgical risk, and on carotid angiography had a 70% occlusion of the carotid artery on the side of the brain that produced the ischaemic symptoms, a 50% occlusion on the contralateral side, and no ulcer in either artery.

3. An explicit definition of appropriateness was agreed to. Appropriateness was judged on a global scale from 1 (inappropriate) to 9 (appropriate). Appropriate was defined as whether the health benefit would be expected to exceed the health risk by a sufficiently wide margin for the procedure to be worth doing. Health was defined in the broadest possible terms and included functioning, pain, worry, disability and death. Cost was explicitly excluded and the physician judges were instructed, when rating appropriateness, to consider the average

patient with the specified clinical characteristics who received care from the average doctor.[7]

4. A panel of 9 physicians was selected to rate the appropriateness of the 864 indications. The panel represented all specialties of medicine concerned with the use of this procedure (not just those who perform the procedure), all regions of the country, and academic and practising physicians. These 9 physicians received the literature review and the set of indications. They revised and rated the indications in the privacy of their homes. The material was returned to RAND where it was computer analysed. All revisions in indications were discussed by telephone with individual panel members, and then a 1½-day panel meeting was held. Each physician at the panel meeting had a form that contained all indications and, for each indication, identified his vote and, anonymously, how the other 8 physicians voted. The chairman of the meeting, who was the physician staff member responsible for the literature review, used a slightly different form. It identified the vote of each panel member by name and showed whether the panel had reached agreement on the appropriateness level for that indication. Before the panel meeting, staff reviewed this printout to see how much agreement and disagreement existed, whether disagreement followed some particular clinical model, and whether the literature could be used to shed light on which clinical model was correct. At the panel meeting, discussions were focused on disagreements and the panellists then re-rated all indications.

For each indication, a determination was made of whether the panel felt use of the procedure for that group of patients was appropriate (median panel rating of 7–9 without disagreement), inappropriate (median panel rating of 1–3 without disagreement) or equivocal (median panel rating of 4–6 or any median with disagreement). Disagreement was defined as occurring when at least three panel members rated the indication 7–9 and at least three members rated it 1–3. The ratings were compared with the literature, subjected to analyses in which appropriateness was regressed on the clinical components of the indications, and sent to all interested parties in an effort to determine their face, content and construct validity.[8,9]

When the ratings were applied to medical record data obtained from a random sample of patients 65 years of age and over who underwent carotid endarterectomy in one of three states in the United States, it was discovered that about one-third of these procedures were judged to be appropriate, one-third equivocal and one-third inappropriate. A similar process demonstrated that one-quarter of coronary angiographies and one-quarter of endoscopies were performed for equivocal or inappropriate reasons.[10] In addition, work in three randomly selected hospitals in one state demonstrated that two-fifths of coronary artery bypass operations were performed for inappropriate or equivocal reasons, and this number varied from 23% to 63% for different hospitals.[11]

Turning our attention now to the outcome of a procedure (ie the desirable and undesirable health consequences), we know that the results obtained vary depending on who carries out the procedure. Luft and others have demonstrated that experience with use of a procedure will for some procedures have an influence on whether a good or a bad outcome is obtained.[12] More strikingly, the Coronary Artery Bypass Surgery Study (CASS) demonstrated, after controlling for a long list of clinical and demographic characteristics of patients, a 20-fold difference in the ratio of observed to expected deaths for coronary artery bypass surgery across 15 academic hospitals.[13] However, what is really not known is whether there are strong positive correlations in outcomes across procedures or hospital departments. Does a physician who removes a gallbladder with an exceptionally low complication rate also have a low recurrence rate when he repairs an inguinal hernia? Is a hospital that has a good track record for coronary artery bypass surgery equally successful in coronary angiography, treating heart attack patients or mending hips? Up to now, it has been difficult to produce evidence to support the notion that a doctor or hospital is good overall as opposed to being good for a particular procedure or disease.[14] Thus, at this moment when trying to relate appropriateness to outcome, it must be done on the basis of an individual procedure or disease.

In summary, there are large differences in appropriateness of use of procedures, and large differences in outcomes of procedures when they are applied. These differences appear to occur at the doctor and hospital level. Are these variations in appropriateness and outcome related to each other?

In particular, at the patient level, after controlling for differences in severity, do doctors who use procedures appropriately perform them better (eg have more patent vessels and fewer deaths 8 years following coronary artery bypass surgery)? Maybe the converse is true. If a physician operates only on appropriate patients, he may do fewer operations, have less experience and perform the operation less well. Maybe all four possible groups exist in roughly equal numbers (ie appropriate operations and good outcomes; appropriate operations but bad outcomes; inappropriate operations but good outcomes; and inappropriate operations and bad outcomes).

Similarly, at a population or community level, after controlling for differences between populations, would people with carotid ischaemic attacks be in better health, as they define it, if carotid endarterectomy were performed only for appropriate reasons (ie if the roughly two-thirds of the operations that were judged to be inappropriate or equivocal were eliminated)?

Answers to these questions are largely unknown, but some weak non-experimental evidence suggests that the answer to the patient-level question might be that there is a weak relationship between appropriateness and outcome at a doctor or patient level. Indirect evidence suggests that, in regard to the population-level question, the provision of only appropriate care may improve health.

As reported earlier, we demonstrated that two-thirds of carotid endarterectomies were performed for inappropriate or equivocal reasons. We also discovered, in a representative community sample, that a stroke in hospital or death within 30 days occurred in 9.8% of the patients. After dividing patients into two groups (those that received appropriate care and those that did not) we found that the complication rate was 8.3% in the former and 10.8% in the latter. Physicians who operated appropriately did achieve somewhat but not substantially better results. This result would indicate that when a patient seeks care or an evaluator measures quality he needs to pay attention to both appropriateness and outcome.[15]

From a population perspective, eliminating inappropriate or equivocal uses of a procedure should improve health. For instance, if one examines the indications that were judged inappropriate or equivocal for coronary artery bypass surgery, they consist of reasons for doing the procedure for which efficacy has not been demonstrated in controlled clinical trials.[16] They involve operating on patients with minimal disease (one or two vessels) who also have minimal symptoms and may not have been tried on medication. The same is true for carotid endarterectomy. An operation was judged equivocal or inappropriate if people with minimal disease were subjected to the procedure. Yet, for both carotid endarterectomy or bypass surgery, the procedure has considerable risks. If inappropriate use were eliminated, this exposure to risk would be reduced and health would most likely improve.

An astute reader of this latter argument will notice that elimination of inappropriate and equivocal procedures has been proposed as the mechanism by which the health of the population would improve. What would happen if the number of apppropriate procedures could be increased (underuse decreased) as the result of more serious case finding or screening? The answer to this question is more tenuous because our analysis of the indications and their ratings demonstrate that physicians accept as appropriate some indications for performing procedures for which there is no supporting scientific evidence. For instance, the panel on endoscopy considered it appropriate to perform endoscopy on almost everybody who presented to a hospital with a GI bleed.[17] Controlled trials in this area, however, have demonstrated that outcome was not improved by use of endoscopy in these patients. In essence, the bias inherent in our process of rating indications may mean that elimination of inappropriate or equivocal uses would improve a population's health, but that increasing appropriate use may only increase health care expenditures.

It is interesting to note that labelling specific indications for use of a procedure that do not have a positive impact on health as appropriate might be less of a problem when British as opposed to American physicians are used as members of the expert panel. In our work with physicians in the Trent region of the UK, they were much less willing than their American counterparts to label the use of a procedure as appropriate in the absence of scientific evidence that supported such an assertion.[18] For instance, when examining coronary artery bypass surgery, of the 305 indications judged appropriate by the US panel, 78 (26%) were so judged by the Trent UK panel. Of the 118 indications judged inappropriate by the US panel, 113 (96%) indications were judged that way by the Trent region panel. When these judgements were applied to real US data, the percentage of coronary artery bypass surgery judged appropriate dropped from 62% to 41%. However, even the judgements of Trent panel members may reflect too great a belief in the efficacy of medical care, and better methods for measuring underuse need to be developed before aggressive case finding based on appropriateness ratings is used as a means to improve health.

It is also almost self-evident that the development of more information to answer questions about the relationship of appropriateness to outcome is imperative. A great many more analytical studies are needed to answer the question. Do doctors who operate or select diagnostic tests appropriately perform them better or obtain better results? The relationship between appropriateness and outcome might differ depending on where the doctor practises (teaching versus non-teaching hospital), country (UK versus USA), specialty, or even on physician or patient characteristics such as age. All sorts of interesting interactions are possible. For instance, teaching hospitals may have physicians who obtain lower complication rates, but they may operate more inappropriately because of the existence of a subconscious need to operate frequently in order to give their residents more experience, to maintain the size of their training programme, or because they are often a court of last resort. Because of this role, physicians in the court may have developed such an enormous belief in themselves and in medicine that they believe they can cure anybody.

To address the relationship at a population level between appropriateness and outcome, carefully prepared population-based studies must be completed. For instance, perhaps all people with transient ischaemic carotid attacks or angina could be identified in a set of defined geographic catchment areas. The areas could be randomised to control or experimental status. In all experimental areas a prospective (before the patient underwent the procedure) evaluation would be made and inappropriate or equivocal endarterectomies (in the case of the transient ischaemic attack) or coronary artery bypass surgery (in the case of angina) would be eliminated. In a subset of the experimental areas, case finding could also be done to identify people who need an endarterectomy or bypass operation and are not being offered it. Different methods of measuring appropriateness could also be used in some experimental areas using a global approach and in others using one based on combining patient preferences with, when possible, literature-derived probability estimates of outcomes. By use of both a cross-sectional and a longitudinal design, the health of people with the target conditions in the experimental and control areas could be compared.

It is feasible to do such experiments and analyses. If we are to improve quality of care we must know more about how to make valid judgements of appropriateness of care and the relationship between appropriateness and outcome. Quality of care will not improve if we increase the number of appropriate procedures performed but perform them in a manner such that complication rates are unacceptably high. On the other hand, even if procedures are performed well, health will not improve unless they are carried out on the people who can benefit from them. For the present, a strategy to improve quality of care must pay attention to, and measure, to the best of our current ability, whether the care provided was appropriate (neither too little nor too much) and whether it was carried out in a manner that would achieve the best health outcome.

References

1. Brook, R.H. (1988) Quality assessment and technology assessment: critical linkages. In *Quality of care and technology assessment* (ed. K.N. Lohr and R.A. Rettig) pp 21–8. Washington, DC: National Academy Press.
2. McNeil, B.J., Pauker, S.G., Sox, H.C. Jr and Tversky, A. (1982) On the elicitation of preferences for alternative therapies. *Preferences for Alternative Therapies*, **306** (21), 1259–62.
3. Brook, R.H., Chassin, M.R., Fink, A. *et al.* (1986) A method for the detailed assessment of the appropriateness of medical technologies. *International Journal of Technology Assessment in Health Care*, **2**(1), 53–63.
4. Brook, R.H. and Lohr, K.N. (1985) Efficacy, effectiveness, variations, and quality: boundary-crossing research. *Medical Care*, **23**, 710–22.
5. Fink, A., Kosecoff, J., Chassin, M.R. and Brook, R.H. (1984) Consensus methods: characteristics and guidelines for use. *American Journal of Public Health*, **74**, 979–83.

6. Merrick, N.J., Fink, A., Brook, R.H. *et al.* (1986) *Indications for selected medical and surgical procedures—a literature review and ratings of appropriateness: carotid endarterectomy* (R-3204/6-CWF/HF/PMT/RWJ). Santa Monica, California: The RAND Corporation.

7. Park, R.E., Fink, A., Brook, R.H. *et al.* (1986) Physician ratings of appropriate indications for six medical and surgical procedures. *American Journal of Public Health*, **76**(7), 766–71.

8. Merrick, N.J., Fink, A., Park, R.E. *et al.* (1987) Derivation of clinical indications for carotid endarterectomy by an expert panel. *American Journal of Public Health*, **77**(2), 187–90.

9. Merrick, N.J., Brook, R.H., Fink, A. and Solomon, D.H. (1986) Use of carotid endarterectomy in five California veterans administration medical centers. *Journal of the American Medical Association*, **256**(18), 2531–5.

10. Chassin, M.R., Kosecoff, J., Park, R.E. *et al.* (1987) Does inappropriate use explain geographic variations in the use of health care services? *Journal of the American Medical Association*, **258**(18), 2533–7.

11. Winslow, C.M., Kosecoff, J., Chassin, M.R. *et al.* (1988) The appropriateness of performing coronary artery bypass surgery. *Journal of the American Medical Association*, **260**(4), 505–9.

12. Luft, H.S., Hunt, S.S. and Maerki, S.C. (1987) The volume–outcome relationship: practice-makes-perfect or selective-referral patterns? *Health Services Research*, No. 22, 157–82.

13. Kennedy, J.W. *et al.* (1980) Multivariate discriminant analysis of the clinical and angiographic predictors of operative mortality from the Collaborative Study in Coronary Artery Surgery (CASS). *Journal of Thoracic and Cardiovascular Surgery*, **80**, 876–7.

14. Richards, T., Lurie, N., Rogers, W.H. and Brook, R.H. (1988) Measuring differences between teaching and nonteaching hospitals (Supplement), *Medical Care*, **26**(5), S1–141.

15. Winslow, C.M., Solomon, D.H., Chassin, M.R. *et al.* (1988) The appropriateness of carotid endarterectomy. *New England Journal of Medicine*, **318**, 721–7.

16. Chassin, M.R., Park, R.E., Fink, A. *et al.* (1986). *Coronary artery bypass graft surgery.* R-3204/2/CWF/HF/HCFA/PMT/RWJ (see Ref. 6).

17. Kahn, K.L., Roth, C.P., Kosecoff, J. *et al.* (1986) *Diagnostic upper gastrointestinal endoscopy.* R-3204/4/CWF/HF/HCFA/PMT/RWJ (see Ref. 6).

18. Brook, R.H., Park, R.E., Winslow, C.M. *et al.* (1988) Diagnosis and treatment of coronary disease: comparison of doctors' attitudes in the USA and the UK. *Lancet*, **i**, 750–3.

6 | Using clinical performance data to stimulate quality improvement

Paul M. Schyve and James S. Roberts

Joint Commission on Accreditation of Healthcare Organizations, Chicago, Illinois, USA

The Joint Commission

In the United States of America, more than 5,200 hospitals are voluntarily surveyed and accredited by the Joint Commission on Accreditation of Healthcare Organizations. The Joint Commission is a private, not-for-profit organisation, the goal of which is to improve the quality of health care provided to the American public by improving the performance of health care organisations. The Joint Commission is not a governmental agency but is sponsored by the major health care professional groups in the United States. Its financial support comes from fees paid by the health care organisations that request survey, and by those who attend Joint Commission educational programmes and purchase Joint Commission publications.

A voluntary accreditation programme for hospitals began in the United States with the Hospital Standardization Program of the American College of Surgeons in 1918. Initiated by this newly formed professional body, the programme established five standards which were used to survey hospitals in an effort to improve the quality of care and to improve the setting in which training of future surgeons was to occur. By 1951 more than half the hospitals in the United States were accredited through this voluntary process. The number of surveys and the cost of conducting them led the American College of Surgeons to work with other professional groups to form the Joint Commission on Accreditation of Hospitals (renamed the Joint Commission on Accreditation of Healthcare Organizations in 1987) to continue the accreditation programme. The original sponsoring organisations, in addition to the American College of Surgeons, were the American College of Physicians, the American Hospital Association, the American Medical Association and the Canadian Medical Association. In 1959 the Canadian Medical Association withdrew from the Joint Commission to form an accrediting body within Canada. The American Dental Association joined the Joint Commission's sponsors in 1979.

The Joint Commission serves as the mechanism by which health care professionals throughout the United States establish standards for, and evaluate, health care organisations. In addition to its sponsoring organisations, the Joint Commission ensures that numerous other major professional groups are represented on its many advisory committees; their counsel and recommendations are thereby incorporated into the work of the Joint Commission.

The Joint Commission is also aided substantially in its work by the input of knowledgeable members of the public. The Board of Commissioners of the Joint Commission, its governing body, has 24 members, of which three are nationally recognised individuals who are not health care professionals and who have the responsibility to bring a broader perspective to Board deliberations. Similarly, virtually all the standing and *ad hoc* advisory committees of the Joint Commission have public members.

As indicated above, the Joint Commission seeks to improve the quality of health care by guiding and encouraging constant enhancement of the work of health care organisations. The Joint Commission does not review the care provided by individual practitioners; that is the responsibility of the organisation being accredited. However, the Joint Commission does examine whether the organisation is reviewing the practitioners' care. By 'organisation' the Joint Commission means both the hospital and its medical staff—all the medical practitioners in the hospital, whether employed or not. The Joint Commission accomplishes its goal through four principal activities.

1. It establishes standards for health care organisations. Currently it has developed standards for seven major types of health care organisation: hospitals, ambulatory health care organisations, hospices, home care, long-term care facilities, managed care systems, and non-hospital organisations providing mental health / substance abuse / mental retardation / developmental disability services.

2. The Joint Commission uses these standards to survey and monitor health care organisations that apply for accreditation survey. Currently the Joint Commission surveys 8,300 organisations and programmes, including more than 80% of the hospitals in the United States. Each organisation is surveyed every 3 years.

3. The Joint Commission uses the results of the surveys to make decisions about accreditation of health care organisations. These decisions are based upon an elaborate set of rules that weight and aggregate the level of compliance with the numerous standards used in

the survey. These summary evaluation decisions fall into one of four categories: accredited without Type 1 recommendations (ie for serious deficiencies); accredited with Type 1 recommendations; conditionally accredited; and non-accredited. Of the 80% of US hospitals surveyed, approximately 2% are non-accredited. Six to eight per cent are conditionally accredited. These hospitals must then file, and receive approval for, a plan of correction, and then demonstrate, through a subsequent on-site focused survey, correction of the serious deficiencies within 6 months. Most of the remainder of the hospitals surveyed (85–90%) are accredited with Type 1 recommendations that must be corrected before the next triennial survey, and are monitored by the Joint Commission through written progress reports or, more likely, on-site focused surveys. Finally, about 5% of hospitals are accredited without Type 1 recommendations.

4. The fourth major activity of the Joint Commission is education. It provides about 250 seminars per year and a large number of publications. The Joint Commission also provides, through a not-for-profit subsidiary (Quality Healthcare Resources), consultation to health care organisations. All these initiatives are designed to help health care organisations improve the quality of patient care that they provide.

The Joint Commission's accreditation is recognised not only by patients in choosing from which organisations to seek services and by private payers (eg Blue Cross) in their consideration of providers for reimbursement, but also by the federal and many state governments in the United States. The federal government recognises accredited hospitals as having met most of the health and safety regulations for participation in the Medicare insurance programme for the elderly and disabled and for participation in the Medicaid insurance programme for the poor. Hospitals that are not accredited must be surveyed by the appropriate governmental agency to be eligible to receive Medicare/Medicaid payments. Similarly, 43 of the 50 United States recognise Joint Commission accreditation for some or all of their quality-related licensure requirements for hospitals. Thus, although the Joint Commission is a private organisation sponsored by the health care professions, its standards and decisions are recognised and used by the public, including the government, for judging the quality of health care organisations and for making decisions about payment eligibility.

Use of outcomes to assess quality of patient care

Since the Joint Commission evaluates and accredits health care organisations, one might wonder why it has become involved in the measurement of patient outcomes. There are two reasons. First, the outcomes of medical care are not the result only of the activities of individual physicians or other individual health care practitioners. Health care today is very complex; it requires the effective interaction of the physician, other practitioners, management, support services and technology. In hospital settings, therefore, the results (outcomes) of intervention are the outputs of the organisation, not just of the physician alone. Second, one of the commitments of health care professionals is to strive to find better ways to treat patients; this is facilitated when health care professionals evaluate what they do, and its results, on an organisational basis, using aggregate data.

Before looking further at the Joint Commission's involvement in measurement of outcomes, it would be useful to reflect on the many outputs produced by a hospital, since it is in understanding these and their relative importance that one begins to grasp the significant challenges faced by hospitals in the United States and all over the world. A partial listing of the many outputs of a hospital would include:

— improved health and well-being;
— stabilised health;
— prevention of future disability or death;
— improved social or family environment;
— efficient use of limited societal resources;
— enhanced community or business productivity;
— employment for the community;
— financial return for investors.

Not only is the variety of outputs evident but it is also clear that there is potential conflict between these outputs. For example, conflict may arise when limited organisational profitability conflicts with the provision of jobs, or when a desire to expand creates a resources drain from existing services, thus jeopardising their quality. The Joint Commission's primary interest is in helping the organisations that it accredits to focus on the outputs which relate to patient outcomes: improved health and well-being; stabilised health; and prevention of future disability and death. While doing so the Joint Commission recognises that an organisation must often meet these objectives while also focusing on other outputs of importance to the organisation.

A primary goal of a health care organisation and its practitioners should be to increase the probability of desired patient outcomes and decrease the probability of undesired outcomes. When patients present to a health care organisation with symptoms or problems, there is most often a germane body of current knowledge related to the causes and treatment of those symptoms. It is the responsibility of the practitioners who care for the patient to apply that knowledge well. The organisation in which the care occurs is responsible for giving proper support to the application of that knowledge by the practitioners. This support requires people, equipment, relevant operating procedures, etc. The current standards of the Joint Commission, developed by the nation's experts, guide the organisation in the functions it must perform to foster and support effective application of the current state of knowledge.

These current standards, and the evaluation process that is driven by them, enable the structures and processes, but generally not the outcomes, of the health care organisation to be assessed. Certainly, the way in which a health care organisation and its individual practitioners increase the probability of desired patient care outcomes and decrease the probability of undesired outcomes is through the specific activities that the organisation and the practitioners carry out. Standards for structure and process examine whether an organisation has mechanisms to ensure that it has the right people and equipment in place to carry out these activities, and whether it has adequately planned to carry them out. Standards of process also examine whether the activities have actually been executed. These standards can therefore indicate primarily whether an organisation is capable of providing quality health care. However, this approach (looking primarily at capability) is no longer sufficient. It is also necessary to examine whether the organisation is effectively carrying out the activities it has planned, and whether that effectiveness is reflected in actual patient care outcomes. Only by looking at the effect of the activities on the probabilities of desired patient care outcomes and undesired outcomes can judgements be made about the actual performance of a health care organisation.

The Joint Commission recognises that the outcomes of patient care provided by an organisation and its practitioners are dependent upon many contributory factors, not all of which are under the control of the organisation or its practitioners. It is evident that the outcomes are dependent upon factors that the organisation and its practitioners can control, eg medical care, nursing care, care given by other individuals, team care, organisational governance, organisational management and support services. However, the outcomes are also dependent upon government policies, the purchasing policies of private organisations such as insurance companies and business, the state of knowledge about the causes and treatments of disease, and the behaviour of patients and their families. None of these factors—and there are surely others—is under the control of the health care organisation and its practitioners. If the quality of health care services is to be assessed accurately and improved, the evaluation of quality must take into account not only both practitioner and organisational factors but also those factors that the organisation and practitioner do not control.

The Joint Commission is now embarked on a long-term applied research and development project, the goal of which is the development of a survey and accreditation process that takes into account the actual performance of a health care organisation, as indicated in part by patient care outcomes, as well as the organisation's capability. We call this research and development project the Agenda for Change. It is designed to create for the Joint Commission greater influence with health care organisations in improving the quality of care. Consistent with the Joint Commission's serving as a mechanism by which health care professionals improve the quality of care, the Agenda for Change is structured as a collaborative effort between the Joint Commission and the health care field. Consequently it includes expert panels of advisers from throughout the United States, local (ie in hospital) alpha and beta test phases, and an assessment of the readiness of health care organisations to make the changes envisaged in the Agenda for Change.

This last assessment is designed to help the Joint Commission time the implementation of the contemplated changes appropriately. There are two potential obstacles to full implementation of these changes:

1. The use of outcome data demands the collection and analysis of aggregate data, and cross-organisational comparisons of organisation-specific data require uniformity in data collection and the construction of large-scale databases. Thus the information systems required for efficient data collection and analysis may need to be improved before full implementation can occur.

2. The most effective use of outcome data to improve the quality of care will require a change in organisational culture. Current quality assurance efforts tend to be focused only on individuals (eg a specific physician) and on deficiencies (eg physician errors). Instead, health care organisations must appreciate how data can be used to improve care rather than just to find mistakes and assign blame—the 'bad apple approach'. Also, they must focus on the continual improvement of quality, and better appreciate all the organisational factors that contribute to quality.

Because these obstacles exist, the Joint Commission is in the process of designing systematic assessments of both, and will use the results to determine the pace at which new outcome measures and standards can be implemented.

Performance monitoring system

The Agenda for Change was initiated in January 1987. In the following 3 years the Joint Commission has devoted its efforts to two component projects: the identification and testing of performance indicators and the development of a new approach to standards. The remainder of this paper will focus primarily on the former.

A key and complex objective of the Agenda for Change is to construct an interactive, indicator-driven information system that is useful in stimulating improvement in the performance of an accredited organisation. By 'interactive' is meant a system in which the Joint Commission will receive information from each accredited organisation, analyse the information, and feed it back to the organisation. These data will be used by the organisation to assess and improve the quality of care it provides, and further feedback will provide to the Joint Commission, over the years, information about which indicators and feedback approaches work best.

The fundamental structure of this performance monitoring process is as follows:

- The health care organisation will assess, using standardised measures —called indicators—developed by the Joint Commission, the outcomes of patient care provided by the organisation. These indicators will be used by the organisation itself as it continually assesses and improves the quality of care it provides.

- Data collected about these indicators will also be sent to the Joint Commission on a quarterly basis and entered into a national database. These data will be accompanied by data about certain covariates that are thought to be related to patient outcomes, such as patient risk factors.

- The Joint Commission will analyse the data in the national database and calculate statistically expected outcomes for each health care organisation, after adjusting for the covariates.

- This comparative information will be fed back to each health care organisation for the health care organisation to use in assessing and improving the quality of care. In addition, the Joint Commission will identify those organisations where performance is a statistical outlier (whether positive or negative) compared with the national data.

- The Joint Commission will assess the effectiveness with which an accredited health care organisation utilises the feedback it receives in improving the quality of care. This effectiveness will be reflected in the accreditation decision about the organisation.

In summary, using a well tested set of measures—indicators—in a Joint Commission monitoring system, the Joint Commission will provide comparative information to the organisation which the organisation will use to assess and change its clinical, managerial, governance and support activities in order to improve its outputs, especially the quality of care it provides.

Indicator development process

The indicator development process involves four phases. The first is the development of proposed indicators by an expert task force. Composed of experts in the specific field under study, the task force first identifies those measures that it believes are related to the quality of patient care. For example, in obstetrics, an expert task force identified, among others, the following patient outcomes that should be measured: number of patients with eclampsia; number of maternal readmissions within 14 days of delivery; number of intrahospital maternal deaths up to and including 42 days postpartum during the primary stay or during a readmission stay; number of discharge diagnoses of birth trauma. Next, the task force defines explicitly the specific data to be collected for the indicator. For example, in the obstetric indicators described above, both 'eclampsia' and 'birth trauma' would be specifically defined. The task force then determines whether the proposed indicator is a sentinel event, ie each case deserves evaluation, or is to be expressed as a rate, ie the rate, rather than an individual event, is what is useful in assessing the quality of care. Next, the task force identifies the rationale for the relationship of each specific proposed indicator to the quality of patient care. It also identifies the potential data sources for each indicator's data (eg medical records, discharge summaries). Finally, the task force identifies those factors that it believes could be related to changes in indicator data: patient-specific factors, practitioner-specific factors, and organisational factors.

In the second phase of the indicator development process, the proposed indicators are pilot tested (alpha test). Currently the Joint Commission is pilot testing indicators in 17 hospitals, soon to be expanded to about 50. The alpha test sites were selected to represent a broad range of hospitals: from small hospitals to large, from rural hospitals to urban, from private hospitals to government hospitals to university hospitals. This testing is designed to determine the face validity of the proposed indicators, whether the required data are available, how expensive it is to collect the data, how accurately the data can be collected, and whether the indicators demonstrate enough variability between organisations to discriminate among organisations. The alpha test has been a highly successful interactive process between the test sites and the Joint Commission. For example, the collection of the full set of obstetric indicators (some of which were listed above) initially took 35 minutes and cost

US$7.76 per case. By the end of the pilot test, collection took [
and approximately US$0.80 per case.

In the third phase of the indicator development process, full testi
(beta test) is undertaken. This testing will begin for the first sets o
indicators (obstetrics and surgical and anaesthesia care) in 1990. Four
hundred hospitals will collect indicator data and send them to the Joint
Commission. The Joint Commission will analyse the data and feed back
comparative data to the beta test hospitals for their use. The Joint
Commission will also further test the interactive data exchange with
hospitals and the utility of the indicators in improving the quality of care.
In addition, all other accredited hospitals will be encouraged to begin
to use the Joint Commission indicators voluntarily and to report to the
Joint Commission on their experiences.

The fourth phase of the indicator development process will be full
implementation in which all accredited hospitals will be required to use
the Joint Commission indicators. Full implementation, expected in
1992, will employ the system of data collection, analysis and feedback
described earlier.

Current status of indicator development

Currently the Joint Commission has completed alpha testing on indicators in obstetrics and anaesthesia care, and these indicators will enter
beta testing in the first half of 1990. Proposed indicators in trauma,
oncology and cardiovascular care have been developed by expert task
forces and are now entering alpha testing in about 50 hospitals.

Beginning in 1990 the Joint Commission plans to initiate additional
task forces to develop further indicators for hospitals in the following
areas:

— Medication usage
— Infection surveillance and control
— Clinical laboratory services
— Imaging services
— Perioperative care

In addition, beginning in 1990 the Joint Commission will establish
expert task forces to begin development of indicators for non-hospital
fields: home care, managed care (HMOs) and mental health care (which
will also include hospital mental health care).

Refocusing accreditation standards

As indicated earlier, a second important objective of the Agenda for
Change is to revise accreditation standards so that they focus more

al and managerial functions that are critical to the
e. In these revisions, two major areas of standards
sed. The first is that of quality improvement, and
th this topic has identified the following concepts
ion into standards:

n quality assessment and improvement, not just

...tioners

— Seeking opportunities to improve quality, not just to identify problems
— Describing, evaluating and improving key quality-related clinical, managerial, governance and support processes
— Broadening and improving the information base used to assess the quality of care, especially the use of feedback from patients
— Improving the capability to analyse, display and use quality-related information to improve the quality of care
— Involving the leaders of the organisation in quality improvement efforts

This last issue—the involvement of the leaders of the organisation in the quality improvement efforts—is the second major area in which standards revisions are currently under way. Successful quality improvement requires that the organisation's governance, managerial and clinical leaders:

— promote attention to quality throughout the organisation;
— become personally knowledgeable about quality improvement concepts and methods;
— explicitly consider quality when making decisions (eg planning, budgeting, allocation of resources);
— seek and use feedback and statistics about quality;
— periodically evaluate their own effectiveness in improving quality;
— ensure the availability of resources and time to assess and improve quality;
— work together to evaluate and improve quality.

Conclusion

The Joint Commission attempts to stimulate US health care organisations to assess and improve continually the quality of patient care they provide. In order to accomplish this goal better, the Joint Commission is developing a system to monitor organisational performance through the use of well tested indicators that will supplement current and new standards which describe those organisational processes that are keys to patient care quality.

7 | Outcomes management and performance indicators

James Coles
CASPE Research, King Edward's Hospital Fund for London
London

The assessment of 'performance' in clinical care is a subject that is liable to raise the blood pressure of even the most easy going clinician, particularly when initiated by a lay manager. Yet managers are even now charged with the responsibility of ensuring that care is appropriate and at least adequately provided, and in the future they may well be expected to account for the outcomes achieved within their units against agreed and specified contracts.

The reasons for clinical apoplexy over performance measures are varied but they include whether non-physicians have the information necessary to make decisions about medical care, the appropriate level at which managers should participate in outcome discussions, the quality of the data used and the correctness of the interpretation put on any messages that appear to arise from their analysis.

The Department of Health's national performance indicators (PIs), now called health service indicators or HSIs,[1] have been criticised in these terms, with most doctors adding that they say next to nothing about quality and are of little relevance to them. On the other hand, more specific patient-based data such as those coming from medical audit studies are difficult to aggregate meaningfully to a level that is of use in strategic resourcing and other similar decision-making processes. Managers faced with decisions concerning whether to invest in one clinical service at the expense of others are left with inadequate means of assessing the overall output of a service (in outcome terms), and the decision is therefore often made on volume considerations alone.

This paper, as well as looking at performance indicators and 'outcomes management' individually, examines the need for a sharing of some outcome (as well as input and throughput) data between clinicians and managers in order to reach a common perspective on the effectiveness of services provided. It does not presume to claim a solution for these complex issues but rather seeks to enhance the debate about how hospitals might ensure that quality is a major focus within any commercially orientated environment in health care.

Performance indicators

What is performance?

Performance is unfortunately an ambiguous word — and not only within the health service. If we ask someone how they would rate the performance of a footballer on a particular occasion, it immediately suggests that a set of criteria exists against which to judge that 'performance'. Establishing such criteria introduces subjective assessments of particular factors and their assimilation into some composite figure. This inevitably leads to the sort of debates and disagreements that occur post-match on most Saturdays. A further example, such as considering the performance of a car, highlights the need to specify the value set in which we are working. For example, is one looking for speed, efficiency (miles per gallon), output in terms of reliability, or quality perhaps in terms of comfort?

Once one has decided on the objectives against which to measure performance, a number of further questions appear. These are shown in Table 1, but highlighting two of them gives a feeling for the complexities surrounding the subject. First, on any specific occasion one needs to decide whether to consider absolute performance or change made over a given period of time. While the former is clearly important in a managerial context, relative movement is often equally so, since one wishes to know the scale of improvement that has been achieved. A poor performer in one year is unlikely to have improved sufficiently to be at the other end of the distribution in the next, whatever effort has been expended in between. The second issue concerns the standard against which performance is to be measured. One may not expect to meet every

Table 1. Some considerations in measuring performance

- Against what objectives are we assessing performance?
- From whose perspective are we measuring performance?
- Are some measures more important than others?
- Is performance absolute or relative over time?
- Do we allow for constraints outside our control?
- What is acceptable variability in performance?

---

target continuously, eg a waiting time of less than x minutes for every outpatient, but rather to be within tolerable limits across a broad spectrum of appropriate measures.

In constructing an indicator of performance therefore one needs to address each of these aspects. Additionally, under a somewhat different formulation, Best[2] has identified three properties that PIs should possess as a minimum:

(i)   they should be performance calibrated, ie a movement in one direction should indicate either better or worse performance;

(ii) such a movement must be subject to unambiguous interpretation and

(iii) must be subject to influence by those whose performance is being judged.

PIs in the National Health Service

The Department of Health's performance indicator package developed out of pioneering work carried out in the late 1970s under John Yates[3] who started presenting back to clinicians and managers comparative information collated from regularly returned statistics. Each measure was presented as a range bar with upper and lower deciles marked and as a histogram showing the variability across the country and the position of the individual district/hospital on the distribution. An important feature of Yates' approach was that the data were sent only to those health authorities who requested it, although by 1987 all but two English districts were receiving the computer discs.

The Department's package[4] increased the number of variables made available in this way and, with a number of other refinements, later introduced an 'expert' system which enabled users to follow a particular logic path through the 400 or so indicators when addressing a particular problem, eg the length of the waiting list for a given specialty. This expert system[5] has to date been taken up by about 80 authorities.

How well do PIs in the NHS measure up to the criteria described earlier? To date they have probably not done very well. Movement in many of the indicators, eg shorter length of stay, higher percentage of home births, increased cost per case, can be considered either good or bad depending on the interpretation. Others of the indicators, eg percentage of joint finance spent on mental illness, can be influenced only partially by health service intervention, or more specifically by the action of managers.

There have been criticisms of the lack of focus in the indicators,[6] although the Department would argue that this was to be locally determined. The guidance in the PI manual specifically adopts a hands-off approach with such references as 'Local information, knowledge and experience are essential to assess the validity of inferences drawn from PIs' and 'PIs provide a starting point for investigation'. While this may have been the intention, some health authorities have rather different experiences of their application. Many of the reviews of PIs have been autocratic and set against non-explicit objectives, with the efficiency perspective dominant and often overriding a realistic assessment of what is achievable. In other words, PIs in application have paid less attention to the local environment than they might have done.

Having been critical of the PI package, I should now perhaps present the other side of the story. In 1987, at the time the Department were formulating their views about the construction of the PI package post-Korner, the Health Service Indicators and Information Branch of the Department commissioned CASPE to undertake a national survey to find out what use was being made of the then current packages and what were the views of the NHS about PIs. A detailed report was produced[7,8] which showed a surprisingly high level of use geographically across districts but in a limited range of applications. These are summarised in Table 2.

Comments were sought about the 'best' features of the packages, and replies focused on the technological advance of providing large amounts of data in an accessible format (on magnetic media rather than in thick book volumes) and on the benefits of having nationwide information. This latter feature, even allowing for inaccuracies and inconsistencies, offered the opportunity to make comparisons across districts on an impartial and objective basis and enabled districts to establish 'benchmarks' or targets for any particular indicator.

Table 2.   Examples of PI use

Most frequent use:

1. Reducing and rationalising services, cost savings
2. Expansions, developments including use of waiting list money
3. Unit/hospital/specialty reviews

Where PIs were most influential:

1. Bed provision and efficient use thereof
2. Nurse manpower issues
3. Medical manpower issues
4. Other manpower issues

Source: CASPE Survey 1987.

The new PI package containing 1987/8 post-Korner data, which is just becoming available (October 1989), has taken into consideration a number of recommendations made in the CASPE report, including the ability to select clusters of districts to examine and to add local data. A start has been made on adding outcome data by including SMRs and avoidable death figures. However, one penalty of the increased level of information (many indicators are available at specialty level) has been that the number of indicators has risen considerably. This has lent weight to another of CASPE's recommendations, namely that busy managers (of all kinds) need assistance in separating the important first-line indicators, relevant to their work, from the vast quantity of data provided.

Developmental work has been undertaken to see whether it is possible to create simple presentations of small groups of indicators based around a subject area, eg maternity, that relate to the responsibilities of specific managers, eg nurse manager in midwifery. We have called such presentations 'templates'. Such an approach may have a wider application in trying to reduce, to manageable proportions, the overwhelming amount of data that would be produced by serious work on outcome measurement and its relationship to inputs and throughput.

Outcomes management

Let us now move to the measurement of outcomes. As mentioned at the beginning, much of the work on the assessment of outcomes in the UK has been undertaken in a sporadic and isolated way by groups of doctors interested in particular clinical areas, with little comparative analysis across sites being possible. Indeed, the latest PI package has only been able to come up with two 'outcome' measures that are widely available on a geographical basis (avoidable deaths and SMRs) plus certain indicators relating specifically to neonates. The situation is of course changing continually and several initiatives are now across district and national boundaries, eg the work of the WHO collaborating centre.

However, in addition to comparative data, managers and clinicians need to possess the ability to bring together outcome measures with information on process and input to address overall issues of effectiveness. Implicit in this last statement is the need to reduce the vast quantity of data to something that is manageable and interpretable, to enable clinicians and managers to share a common perspective on the means to achieving a common end—better health care for the individual patient. Paul Ellwood has described our need for a common perspective as requiring 'a central nervous system'.[9] His assessment, although

Table 3.   Features of outcomes management[9]

1. Greater reliance being placed on standards and guidelines that physicians can use in selecting appropriate interventions
2. Routine and systematic measurement of the functioning and well-being of patients along with disease specific clinical outcomes at appropriate time intervals
3. Pooled clinical and outcome data on a massive scale
4. Analysis and dissemination of results from the segment of the database most appropriate to the concerns of each decision maker

couched in US terms of HMOs and 'corporate medicine', makes familiar reading in the UK, with

— patients worried about the sensitivity of quality of care to the level of resources available;

— 'payers' worried about variations in practice and performance between geographic areas;

— difficulties of accurate prognosis as medical complexity increases, and primary physicians concerned about recognising the broader needs of patients;

— information systems that increasingly record what was done to patients and the cost thereof, but not why it was done or the outcome.

His suggestion following this analysis was to develop 'a technology for collaborative action' between all interested parties, drawing on four facets of health care information technology (as shown in Table 3) that are becoming rapidly more practicable and acceptable.

As Ellwood recognised, however, there are still problems to be overcome such as the strength of the causal link between medical care and measures of well-being, the reliability and sensitivity of patients' subjective opinions, and the lack of a denominator that includes patients who do not make contact with the health care system. Outcome information is likely to remain imperfect but, as Ellwood acknowledged, the most immediately realisable benefits are likely to occur in the subjective areas by creating 'a sense of participation, a dispelling of suspicion and progress toward a fairer, more effective health care system'.

An approach to outcomes management in the UK

At about the same time as the seeds of Ellwood's ideas were germinating in the US, CASPE Research were putting forward proposals to the

Department of Health[10] identifying the need to develop a range of output measures to match and enhance the information that would become available from the resource management systems. Like Ellwood, we were concerned lest health authorities should be assessed solely on grounds of efficiency and throughput without any evaluation of the quality of care and outcome. As a result of our proposals we are currently working with a number of health authorities on the use of process quality measures, indices of patient satisfaction, and with the Newcastle health authority on the development of 'short-term outcome indicators'. A fourth area examining a population-based access and coverage measure has not been funded to date.

Concentrating on our outcomes work, the Freeman Hospital at Newcastle was chosen partly because a resource management database containing reliable patient-based data on the process of care was being developed, but also because of the very substantial support that our proposals had received from the clinicians there.

The study, which was set up as a feasibility study in the first place to cover two conditions in depth and to develop ideas in a further four, started last autumn. Following the piloting of data capture systems, routine recording began in January 1989.

Currently (October 1989) the project has reached the stage where information is being presented back to clinicians about patients whose initial contacts occurred in the first four months of 1989 and who have been followed through to three months post-operation or post-contact.

A prime objective of the study is to establish a system of data gathering and information presentation, and reporting about outcomes that will be acceptable to clinicians and managers. The need to relate outcomes to the use and availability of resources is also recognised, and mechanisms are being created to bring these two separate databases together to assist discussions. A further objective of the study is to look for commonalities that might apply across conditions or even specialties, since it would seem impracticable to maintain different data protocols for each condition or for strategic decisions to be influenced by diverse messages emanating from a range of outcome methodologies.

With this in mind, it is pleasing to note that our conceptual framework has produced the need for data elements similar to those collected by the much larger medical outcomes study in the US as recently described by Tarlov *et al.*[11] Since the scope of our project is only concerned with outcomes following a contact with secondary care, it is particularly important for us to control for patients presenting at different stages of their condition and with different personal backgrounds. We are therefore collecting a range of pre-morbid patient-based factors, including demographic details, presence of co-morbidities, indications for surgery and time since diagnosis. Information on major events during the patient episode, ie process variables, is being obtained from the administrative computer systems that have existed for some time, while more detail in this area will become available as the resource management case mix computer system develops.

Outcome measurement itself has many dimensions and we are trying to collect data across a number of these. The dimensions chosen were changes in symptomatology and clinical indicators, changes in functional capacity, movements in measures of well-being (health status and patients' perceptions), and post-discharge complications. Similarly, to Ellwood and Tarlov *et al.* we believe it to be important to obtain a patients' perspective on the outcome of care as well as movement in clinical indicators etc. Unlike the US medical outcomes study, we are not currently measuring patient satisfaction at the Freeman Hospital (we are working in this area with a number of other health authorities[12]), but we are making extensive use of patient feedback through interviews and questionnaires and the use of existing tools such as the Nottingham Health Profile (NHP)[13] or the Sickness Impact Profile (SIP).[14]

Figure 1 shows the basic inpatient review model which we are using

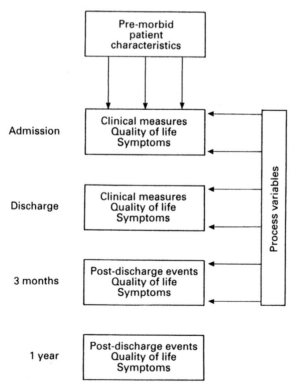

Fig. 1. *Inpatient review model.*

for relatively short-stay acute episodes of care. Our initial work in the acute area has focused on cholecystectomy. On admission, patients are identified by a research nurse and given a self-administered questionnaire to be completed before surgery, the nurse giving help and advice on its completion if necessary. This contains questions about the presence (or lack) of symptoms associated with the problem, a general health status measurement (Nottingham Health Profile) and an overall assessment of one's health. Clinical details, including the indications for admission or surgery, the existence of co-morbidities and current drug therapy, are obtained from the clinical notes by the nurse. In the case of surgery, a further short questionnaire is completed by the operating surgeon, clinically summarising operative and post-operative events or complications.

Three months following discharge the patient receives a postal questionnaire, to be self-administered, replicating the one received on admission but adding questions about whether the patient has had any contact with the health service since discharge relevant to the problem under consideration. Validation checks on these data have been undertaken by home visits to a random sample of patients by an independent member of the research team and the use of a structured interview. Also, an independent search of these patients' notes has been undertaken to look for additional clinical details and post-operative information.

The model for chronic conditions that are largely outpatient-based, eg non-insulin-dependent diabetes, is slightly different, with attempts being made to collect data at each patient contact. Additionally, in this instance, there is a further dimension being monitored. This tries to assess the degree to which patient education has been successful in changing lifestyle or attitude, and whether this has led to improved control.

With data collection starting only in early 1989, analyses at this stage can be no more than illustrative. Of 41 patients who had a cholecystectomy in the 4-month period between mid-January and mid-May, 13 have had subsequent contact with the health service directly related to surgery. Three of these had been re-admitted. On the simple self-assessed health rating, patients were asked to record their overall health as poor, fair, good and very good, both before and 3 months after their surgery. Of the 39 patients who responded, 22 reported improvements in their general health and 12 reported no change. Of course the interpretation of such a response, particularly in a small sample, is difficult since unrelated factors may have affected the patient's general health, or indeed their subjective perception may have changed over time. The value and validity of this measure will be examined over the course of the project.

Table 4. Presence of symptoms pre-operatively and at 3 months follow-up in cholecystectomy patients

Symptom/problem	Not reported pre-op or at 3 months	Present pre-op only	Present at 3 months only	Present pre-op and at 3 months
Use of tablets	26	12	2	1
Flatulence	13	14	4	10
Distension	16	14	3	8
Vomiting	17	21	1	2
Bowel problems	24	2	10	5
Appetite	21	8	7	5
Fatty food intolerance	11	19	2	9

Table 4 shows in greater detail patients' perceptions of how the presence of symptoms changed during the same 3-month period. It shows that symptom relief has been found to be greatest in the areas of vomiting, intolerance to fatty foods and the use of regular analgesia. Flatulence has shown itself somewhat resistant to change in some cases, while bowel problems may be adversely affected by surgery.

The use of a general health status measure, in this case the Nottingham Health Profile (NHP), has shown a close relationship between its aggregate score and the change expressed by the overall health assessment. As shown in Table 5, of the seven dimensions in the NHP, significant improvements have been noted in energy, pain, emotional reactions, lifestyle and, to a lesser extent, sleep. The mobility dimension, however, suggests reduced mobility in a fair number of patients 3 months post-operatively, and this will be monitored through to the 12-month stage. Not surprisingly perhaps with this condition, the majority of patients felt that there had been no change in their level of social isolation.

We are only just beginning to get outcome information from the database, but to date progress has been promising. Data capture has been achieved in a robust and sustainable manner, with few problems of interpretation and within limited resources. On inspection, the information has face validity and also meets other validity checks including personal interviews and independent case-note reviews. Five dimensions of the NHP appear sensitive to changes occurring during a cholecystectomy episode, as does the overall symptomatology of a patient. The presentation of individual symptoms varies quite widely across cases and is therefore less useful.

Table 5.   Changes in a general health status measure (NHP) (pre-operatively to 3 months follow-up) in cholecystectomy patients

Dimension	No. of patients reporting			NHP scores	
	Improved	Unchanged	Worse	Pre-op	At 3 months
Energy	21	18	2	35.7	15.1[a]
Pain	23	13	5	24.7	12.7[a]
Emotional reactions	23	14	4	15.8	6.0[a]
Sleep	23	10	8	26.4	15.2[a]
Social isolation	5	32	4	6.4	4.3
Mobility	12	20	11	12.2	12.3
Lifestyle	21	14	6	22.0	10.8[b]

$n = 41$: [a]$p < 0.01$; [b]$p < 0.05$.

Having established a dataflow, we are now starting to review the information with the clinicians concerned. This should identify redundant elements within the data, ie those providing no additional or interpretable information with regard to outcomes. Additionally, we hope to begin a process of defining, and refining, standards of expected outcomes against which consultants can review the information.

Bringing the ideas together

A major disadvantage of our study is the small scale on which it is based. Working on a few conditions within a single hospital, it will require some considerable time to build up a database upon which statistically meaningful conclusions can be based. Replication in other sites throughout the UK is highly desirable but will need to attract funding.

The medical outcome study in the US has not suffered from this constraint and recruited more than 500 doctors to its study in three cities across the US. Over 2,000 patients suffering from a number of chronic tracer conditions were followed for a period of 2 years and their health and well-being were measured at 6-monthly intervals during this time.

Across studies[11,15] there is a growing consensus about how we might conceptualise outcomes in the short to medium term that could be useful in informing resourcing and other decisions. The need to record patient characteristics such as co-morbidities and to link process and outcome variables, as well as a requirement to measure the various dimensions of outcome giving due weight to the patient's role in assessing them, are all now gaining acceptance. There is still a healthy debate about the advantages of particular instruments in measuring each of the dimensions, and much experimentation will occur before any agreement is reached here. It may be too much to expect that one instrument for measuring, say, functional status will find favour across specialty and geographical boundaries, but one would hope that, if this is the case, results from different instruments will be interpretable against an agreed standard.

While a framework for considering outcome measurement is gradually being proposed, the method by which outcome information can be related to structure and process variables (including cost information) is less well developed. It is perhaps in this area that outcomes management can draw on some of the stronger features of the approaches developed within the UK performance indicator packages. The provision of a statistical distribution for each indicator would give the clinician a reference set for comparison (assuming, of course, that the distribution only contained appropriate and valid comparators), while an expert system approach would allow one to examine the relationship between risk factors, process and outcome variables.

However, as all this information becomes available, clinicians and managers will be faced with the same problems as PIs have posed, namely to reduce it to manageable subsets that address specific areas, eg one specific diagnosis or a coherent group thereof, or particular issues, eg the effect of providing more resources on outcomes. To tackle this problem, we first proposed the development of a template approach (similar to the PI work described above), reproduced in part in Fig. 2.[16] This tries to bring together, for a particular condition, a limited number of important and relevant structure, process and outcome variables, and displays for each a distribution obtained nationally or from relevant peer groups. Using this as guidance, clinicians and managers could derive an 'expected range' for their service, bringing in local demographic and other factors, and compare their current performance against this. Such comparisons could form a basis for service planning discussions between clinicians and managers about changes in resourcing levels and in clinical practice, and their effect on the provision of services.

This, of course, is only one approach but it would seem to me that technological advances in information handling have been successfully applied to the administrative databases upon which PIs are based and could be applied to more clinically oriented databases also. As agreement grows on the type of data that we might collect to analyse outcomes, perhaps we should be heeding Ellwood's call to accelerate the process by 'adding a uniform set of life measures as a new data element to any

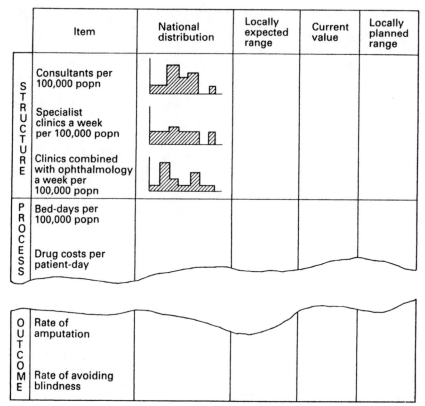

	Item	National distribution	Locally expected range	Current value	Locally planned range
S T R U C T U R E	Consultants per 100,000 popn				
	Specialist clinics a week per 100,000 popn				
	Clinics combined with ophthalmology a week per 100,000 popn				
P R O C E S S	Bed-days per 100,000 popn				
	Drug costs per patient-day				
O U T C O M E	Rate of amputation				
	Rate of avoiding blindness				

Fig. 2. *Example of service based 'template' for diabetes.*

pre-existing computerised clinical data base that has the capacity to relate clinical observations to outcomes'.[9]

Acknowledgement

The author gratefully acknowledges the funding for the Newcastle Outcomes Study received from the Research Management Division, Department of Health, and the continued support of clinicians and managers at the Freeman Hospital.

References

1. Department of Health (1989) *Health service indicators: guidance—dictionary.* London: HMSO.
2. Best, G. (1983) Performance indicators: a precautionary tale for unit managers. In *Effective unit management* (ed. H.I. Wickings) pp 62–85. London: King Edward's Hospital Fund.

3. Yates, J. and Vickerstaff, L. (1982) Inter-hospital comparisons in mentally handicapped. *Mental Handicap*, **10**, 45–7.
4. Department of Health and Social Security (1983) *Performance indicators: national summary for 1981.* London: HMSO.
5. Department of Health and Social Security (1988) *Logical structure of an expert system for Korner-based performance indicators.* London: Arthur Young Management Consultants.
6. McGuire, A. (1986) Economic efficiency and performance indicators. *Hospital and Health Services Review*, March, 72–3.
7. Jenkins, L., Bardsley, M., Coles, J. *et al.* (1987) *Use and validity of NHS performance indicators: a national survey.* London: CASPE Research.
8. Jenkins, L., Bardsley, M., Coles, J. and Wickings, H.I. (1988) *How did we do? The use of performance indicators in the National Health Service.* London: CASPE Research.
9. Ellwood, P.M. (1988) Shattuck lecture: Outcomes management—a technology of patient experience. *New England Journal of Medicine*, **318**, 1549–56.
10. Mills, I. (1987) Getting there. *Health Services Journal*, 16 July, 822.
11. Tarlov, A.R., Ware, J.E., Greenfield, S. *et al.* (1989) The medical outcomes study: an application of methods for monitoring the results of medical care. *Journal of the American Medical Association*, **262**, 925–30.
12. Kerruish, A., Wickings, H.I. and Tarrant, P. (1988) Information from patients as a management tool: empowering managers to improve the quality of care. *Hospital and Health Services Review*, April, 64–7.
13. Hunt, S.M., McEwen, J. and McKenna, S.P. (1984) Perceived health: age and sex comparisons in a community. *Journal of Epidemiology and Community Medicine*, **38**, 156–60.
14. Bergner, M., Bobbitt, R.A. and Carter, B. (1981) The sickness impact profile: development and final testing of a health status measure. *Medical Care*, **19**, 787–805.
15. Neal, D.E., Ramsden, P.D., Sharples, L. *et al.* (1989) Outcome of elective prostatectomy. *British Medical Journal*, **299**, 762–7.
16. Coles, J. and Wickings, H.I. (1985) *The ethical imperative of clinical budgeting.* Nuffield/York Portfolio No. 10 (ed. A.J. Culyer). Oxford: Nuffield Provincial Hospitals Trust.

8 | Measurement of outcomes in general practice

D.H.H. Metcalfe
Department of General Practice, University of Manchester

It has usually been safe to assume that the goal of medical care is altruistic, and its objectives, albeit unstated, to save life, ameliorate suffering, improve function or protect from disease. Today the complexity of the needs for medical care and the multiplicity of technical interventions available make the measurement of outcomes essential as a basis for rational and ethical choices of treatment. As clinicians we have a duty to examine the effectiveness of the care we provide. It is important that politico-economic constraints are not allowed to distort the process.

In this paper I describe the opportunities for outcome measurement in general practice, and the problems encountered when applying them. The essential difference between general practice and the specialties is the breadth of the mixture of cases encountered, and the range of the natural history of diseases with which it is concerned. There can be no argument about the necessity for measuring outcome in general practice: while every working day there are 109,000 inpatients in care, and 151,000 outpatients seen, 750,000 people a day are seen in general practice. Of course much care of patients, in both acute and chronic conditions, is shared between general practitioners and hospital-based specialists. If we are to measure effectiveness in the National Health Service, we will have to do a lot of it in general practice.

Definition

Outcomes are defined as the change in health status that results from medical interventions, or the deliberate decision not to intervene (see Fig. 1). They cannot therefore be measured unless the intervention is accurately described. The description of the intervention should include its explicit objectives, so that the end state can be compared with what was intended, and unintended change identified. The use of the term 'health status' as the subject for end-point assessment conforms to WHO

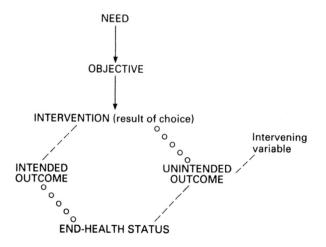

Fig. 1

definitions in that it goes beyond the presence or absence of disease by
including psychological and social well-being.

Purpose of outcome measurement

There are four reasons why we need to be able to measure outcomes:

— To be more objective in our assessment of our patients' progress and
   the effectiveness of our management (and to validate our diagnoses)
— To be able to compare the effectiveness of one treatment with that of
   another
— To validate the process criteria developed for audit
— To be able to assess cost-effectiveness

Our first concern as clinicians must be with the first two purposes:
more valid, and reliable outcome measures should be everyday tools of
the trade. As clinical audit becomes established as a mainstream activity,
rather than an interest of a minority, we must make sure that process
criteria (which are the most tempting to establish and apply) are justified
by measurable improvements in outcome. Efficiency can only be assessed
when care has been shown to be effective, and cost can only be linked to
effectiveness if the latter can be measured. Audits based on comparisons
of process costs regardless of effectiveness would be a disaster.

Needs to be met by general practitioners

General practice aims to meet five main needs in its registered populations:

— Immunisation and screening

— Exclusion of illness

— Early diagnosis

— Management of chronic disease (including psychiatric and psychosocial distress)

— Terminal care

These are all needs for which there are clear-cut interventions which by
definition must have outcomes, and these in turn should be measurable.
Moreover, they are all tasks for which we have a clear-cut mandate from
individual patients and the public at large.

Then there are all the other odd jobs that the great and the good have
added to that role, whether or not there is evidence that they are effective,
whether or not we have the skills and resources, whether or not we have
a mandate from our registered populations, and regardless of the
opportunity costs! These include things like health education, health
promotion, well-person clinics, entrance health assessments, and the
rest. They have much more diffuse and unformed objectives, and less-
defined interventions.

Technical problems

There are five problems to be overcome if outcome measurement is to
be generally applicable, valid and reliable.

1. *Differentiation between acute disease treatment and chronic illness
management.* Measurements of outcome must be valid, ie they must
measure progress toward the goals of care. When these are complex,
addressing several needs, several measures of outcome will be needed.
For this reason, it is important to differentiate between treatment and
management. 'Treatment' describes a relatively circumscribed range of
technical interventions focused primarily on the pathophysiology:
disease-centred care. 'Management' describes the range of interventions
directed to the totality of the patient's ill-health, physical, social and
psychological: patient-centred care. Disease-centred care is appropriate
in the inpatient care of patients, particularly those with acute illness, not
least because they are in no position to try to maintain their normal social
function. In general practice, and especially in the care of chronic and
psychiatric illness, the objectives, and therefore the measurements of
outcome, must be management orientated and patient centred.

Perhaps we should adopt the rule that only when the patient is non-
autonomous, for example when he is in hospital, can care be purely
disease-centred, and outcomes measured in pathophysiological terms.

When the patient is autonomous, and particularly when he is in his normal environment, care must be patient-centred, and outcomes measured in terms of health status.

2. *Establishment of explicit objectives (where traditionally the profession has preferred to leave them implicit).* The lack of explicit objectives precludes rational choice of outcome measures in all but the simplest of cases. If what the doctor is trying to achieve is not known, how does one know what to measure? Without explicit and agreed objectives, judgements may be made on the wrong parameters.

3. *Achievement of a comprehensive definition of the intervention in those situations where it is complex.* In acute illness, or in the inpatient episodes of a chronic disease, the interventions are discrete and relatively simple, because they mostly have short-term goals. Analysis of consultations has shown that in the surgery (and probably in outpatients) the intervention is a mixture of contributions, all of which are valued by patients, and therefore might be expected to contribute to improved health status. These include taking the patient seriously, explaining, reassuring, agreeing goals and plans, supporting or training lay carers, prescribing, and referring for specific treatment. All of these may have an appreciable effect on the patient's subsequent well-being; which one did the good?

4. *Development and selection of measurements of physical status, feelings and function which are valid, reliable and applicable.* Health is broader than the absence of disease; the concept includes feelings and functional capacity. Care by general practitioners is directed at all components of health, using different sorts of interventions for each.

Many components of physical status are amenable to measurement; examples include thyroid-stimulating hormone levels, peak flow, blood pressure, or joint mobility. Imaging and endoscopy are available for the inspection of lesions. These are comfortably 'scientific' and 'objective', and we set great store by them, but such measurements are only part of the sick person's global health status.

Relief of symptoms is an important objective, but reduction in intensity of symptoms must be assessed subjectively, by the patient. These are partly dependent upon changes in mood which may themselves be the result of confounding variables, such as difficulty in getting an appointment.

Measures of activities of daily living (ADL) are more objective to the extent that they are assessed by an observer rather than by the patient, but they still depend on that observer's subjective judgement of the extent to which the patient's functions conform to the descriptions in the scales. Moreover, these measures have been shown to be affected by other components of the illness such as the amount of pain being experienced at the time of measurement.

Subtler subjective changes in self image and self confidence, while important components of well-being and therefore goals of good comprehensive care, are even more difficult to measure reliably.

The plethora of scales for measuring personal and social function, and the extensive literature assessing their validity and reliability, attest to the fact that this is not a simple or easy field. Those measures that stand up well to evaluation seem to require fairly expert administration by workers with trained skills in social science.

5. *Application of such measures at an appropriate time after the intervention or in the natural history of the disease.* Lastly decisions have to be made about when to measure outcome. Discharge or attendance at a follow-up clinic offer easy and sensible 'end points' at which to assess the outcome after inpatient care. Except in simple acute conditions, however, this may not be the appropriate moment in the natural history of the illness to judge the effectiveness of the care provided. Prudence dictates as long an interval as possible between the intervention and the measurement of outcome, in order to give the maximum time for benefit to accrue, and for unsought events to occur. The longer the measurement is left, however, the more vulnerable is the connection between intervention and outcome to intervening variables.

General practice tasks, objectives and measurements

Listing the tasks of general practice undertaken to meet the multiplicity of needs of patients will provide a framework for developing, choosing and applying outcome measures.

— Primary prevention

— Secondary control (screening and case finding)

— Exclusion

— Care of acute disease

— Care of chronic illness

— Care of psychiatric illness

— Terminal care

Prevention (Table 1)

The outcomes of preventive care are not measurable in individuals because they are non-events! They are only measurable in terms of the reduced incidence of the index disease in the populations concerned, which may have to be large if the condition is relatively rare. Because of this, there is a tendency to measure intermediate outcomes such as population coverage, which is really a process variable. While convenient, this invalidates the use of intermediate outcomes for assessment of cost effectiveness, because the cost of coverage is seldom proportional to the cost of saving each case. Moreover, the use of coverage as an outcome measure precludes the chance of investigating some unwanted effects of screening which are costs to the patient: anxiety about needing the tests; anxiety when waiting for the results; and the trauma of false positives.

Table 1. Prevention

Objectives:	Primary prevention by removal or neutralisation of causal factors Secondary prevention by early diagnosis (where earlier means better)
Outcome measures:	Primary: incidence in population Secondary: death rate or serious complication rate in population

Exclusion of significant illness (Table 2)

A very large proportion of new presentations to general practitioners are for reassurance: what, with hindsight and expertise, we may regard as 'trivial' was worrying enough to the patient to make him come to see us. Exclusion of serious illness, perhaps the most important clinical task of the general practitioner, the real 'gatekeeper' role, requires proper history taking, examination, and sometimes investigation, as a basis for reliable reassurance, which is a major intervention in itself.

Exclusion also has as its outcome a non-event: the illness which the patient explicitly or implicitly feared is not present and does not supervene. The desired outcome is an improvement in health that comes from transferring the patient's health status from worried well to unworried well, but since the grateful patient disappears this outcome is difficult to measure! Follow-up audits could reveal failure by identifying people who had had their non-medical conditions medicalised (false positives), and those in whom serious illness which could have been spotted supervenes.

Table 2.   Exclusion of serious illness

Objective:	Reliable (ie safe) reassurance
Outcome measures:	Absence of subsequent disease for which presenting complaint could have been harbinger Subjective reduction in anxiety in the patient (where anxiety has been the reason for presentation)

Treatment of acute illness or trauma (Table 3)

Acute illness may be managed by treatment and advice, possibly with support from allied professions, or by referral to specialist care.

Acute care has simple objectives which seldom need to be made explicit: it is disease-centred, and is usually evaluated by measurement of physical parameters, or simple assessment of physical capability. Restoration of function, however, depends not only on physical but also on psychological and social parameters, eg self confidence and opportunities for employment.

Table 3.   Acute physical illness or trauma

Objective:	Removal or correction of disease process; repair of trauma, restoration of function
Outcome measures:	Presence or absence of pathology Recovery or non-recovery of function

Management of patients with chronic illness (Table 4)

The pathophysiology of chronic disease dictates the objectives in terms of the reversal, control or slowing down of the disease process. The interventions are those of technical medicine, and outcomes are measured in terms of the progress of the disease process. Distress, including loss of self image, or even of acceptable body image, and frustration with disability must be identified and reduced, by controlling symptoms, counselling and support, including support for carers. The outcome of these interventions can be measured by symptom scores, health diaries or general scales like the Nottingham Health Profile or the Sickness Impact Profile.

Objectives in the domain of function are directed to recovery or maintenance of self care, occupational and household capability, and social interaction. Interventions will include appliances, re-housing, training, nursing and specific therapies. The outcomes must be measured by observers rating the patient's behaviour in these fields.

Table 4. Chronic physical illness

Objectives:	Control of disease process
	Reduction of subjective distress
	Restoration or maintenance of function
Outcome measures:	Objective measures of pathophysiology
	Subjective measures of experience
	Objective measures of function

Psychological illness (Tables 5 and 6)

Psychological disease varies from florid psychosis to normal reactions to social stress. The whole range is seen in general practice.

At the psychotic end of the spectrum, the illnesses conform to the pattern of relapsing chronic physical diseases, but without easily measured parameters of status or progress. With so little understanding of the nature of these diseases, the care in the acute phase is essentially a holding operation, using drugs and surveillance. In the chronic phase, care is designed to maintain calm while restoring social function. Family and other carers are a particularly important resource, but also have their own needs, for support if not care, so their function and feeling should be the subject of outcome measurement if the psychotic patient's care is being fully evaluated. The difficulty in applying such instruments in these patients is, of course, that the very nature of the illness makes the principal witness unreliable. Nevertheless, there are a variety of interview schedules and behavioural rating scales in use which have been shown to have acceptable reliability; the main problem is with

Table 5. Psychological illness at psychosis level

Objectives:	Protection from self harm
	Reduction of distress
	Support for family/carers
Outcome measures:	Self harm happens or does not happen
	Distress estimated by observer or recorded by patient (but patient's illness may make him unreliable witness)
	Family/carers' expression of satisfaction with the extent to which their perceived needs were met

validity. There is considerable argument about whether they measure what is going on in the patient's head.

At the emotional dysfunction end of the spectrum of psychological illness, the natural history is much less predictable, and the objectives for care therefore pragmatic. Standardised psychiatric questionnaires such as the General Health Questionnaire, and interview schedules are useful in this area, particularly in depression, which is a more clear-cut entity.

Table 6.   Psychological illness at neurosis level

Objectives:	Reduction of distress
	Restoration of self management
	Improvement of self image
Outcome measures:	Distress recorded by patient
	Personal and social function measurement
	Self image assessed by observer

Care of the dying (Table 7)

Terminal illness requires a balance of interventions with objectives which include control of symptoms, maintenance of personal and social function, and the achievement of acceptance of impending death. Here the difficulty is that the most sensitive indicator of outcome is the evidence of the patient himself, but most doctors would be hesitant to submit their dying patients to assessments of symptoms, function and feelings, especially before they had come to terms with impending death. Relatives too are unlikely to be objective, having their own needs. Sensitive and acceptable studies have been done by social scientists on a research basis. Spending unhurried time with a dying patient seems to be the most valuable form of care, but to incorporate outcome measures routinely into terminal care would be difficult.

Table 7.   Terminal illness

Objectives:	Symptom control
	Maintenance of function
	Achievement of acceptance (peace of mind)
Outcome measures:	Symptom assessment by patient, principal carer or professional observers
	Assessment of daily living/social function, by patient and carers
	Assessment of peace of mind by patient and carers

Doctors, science and objectivity

Faced with uncertainty, and dogged by failure, in that all our patients eventually die, the medical profession takes refuge in its scientific basis. It is comfortable with measurements which it sees as reliable and objective, like laboratory results and images, even if they are not particularly valid! Here the problem concerns the concept of reliability, which is usually seen as generalisability and predictiveness. While these are important in studies of causality, or in comparisons of treatment, the fact that every human being is unique means that, in many other sorts of health service research, generalisability is irrelevant. Methodologies which strive after the wrong sort of reliability may have reduced validity as a result. Schön[1] has pointed out that professions may be based on what he called the hard high ground of laboratory science but practise in the marshes of uncertainty and pragmatism! In difficult situations, physicians tend to pretend that they are still in the cool, clean laboratory, regardless of the multiplicity of uncontrollable variables, or they may select only those components of the problem that are susceptible to what they see as rigorous examination, and leave the rest untreated. If we are to measure outcomes in a valid, and therefore useful, way we must learn to do so where we are, rather than where we would like to be! As soon as we accept that outcomes are concerned with parameters beyond the simple measures of physiological activity, such as functions and feeling, we must overcome the medical profession's remarkable reluctance to learn from anyone outside its ranks, and seek help from behavioural and social scientists, who have been working hard in this area for a long time. We may not like their jargon—and they may not like ours—but we should respect their realism, in that they recognise that their work is essentially concerned with human experience, and is therefore done 'out in the marshes'. The reliability of their measurements may be a bit muddy, but their validity is commendable. In particular, social scientists have demonstrated that the parameters that we need to be able to measure as we strive to evaluate care are not independent of each other: function and feeling affect each other. We are beginning to see that experience and human response affect our physiology too. The subject of care is not a system or organ, but a person, and the effectiveness of care must therefore be measured comprehensively, using unfamiliar and uncomfortable instruments from colleagues outside medicine. The scholarliness of their efforts to attain reliability without sacrificing validity puts some of our efforts to shame. In an effort to make their work accessible to clinicians, my colleague Dr David Wilkin is about to publish an annotated review of measures appropriate to primary care.

Questions

Five questions need to be answered by general practitioners and family practitioner committees:

1. Which of the clinical activities described should be evaluated, internally or externally? (and if any activity should not be evaluated, should it be undertaken at all?).

2. How many examples of each category of care should be subjected to outcome measurement, and which ones? Can 'tracer' conditions be a reliable indicator of effectiveness in other similar situations?

3. How often should such measurements be made, especially in view of the problems of identifying appropriate times in the natural history of disease?

4. Who should evaluate categories of care—general practitioners or social scientists?

5. What resources, from within or without the practice, should be dedicated to measurement of outcome, and what opportunity costs are containable?

The temptation, of course, is to develop measurements of outcome for easily identified and 'important' interventions, and not for the rest of the protean activities of the general practitioner. To succumb to this would not only forfeit the chance of examining the overall effectiveness of the primary care sector, but might actually skew the pattern of care provided. It is conceivable that some doctors would begin to concentrate their efforts on conditions amenable to outcome measurement, while others might take avoiding action by selective referral. If measures of outcome are to be applied externally to evaluate general practice, the application of only those instruments from bioscience that are used to measure physical status will result in a corresponding bias in the way general practitioners set their objectives and provide care. Political and economic pressures for a 'quick fix' could have serious effects on the sensitivity and comprehensiveness of care.

Conclusions

General practice needs to be able to measure outcomes just as much, and for the same reasons, as the other clinical disciplines. The wide variety of tasks and the multiplicity of the domains in which improvement is attempted, which characterise general practice, necessitate the development of a correspondingly wide range of measuring instruments if validity is to be achieved. There are few practicable (ie economical and reliable) measures currently available in the domains of function and feeling. The need is for the development of a comprehensive set of economical, practicable, valid and reliable instruments. This would be a most appropriate task for academic departments of general practice, were they to have anything approaching reasonable financial support.

Reference

1. Schön, D.A. (1984) The crisis of professional knowledge in the pursuit of an epistemology of practice. Harvard Business School: 75th Anniversary Colloquium on Teaching by the Case Method.

nptom severity, aspects of daily living, personal and social in-
dence, special services required, cost — the possible list of outcome
ires is sizeable and arguable. The conclusion of this conference is
itcome assessment, if it is to reflect the subtlety of what is involved
typical doctor–patient diagnostic and therapeutic exchange, will
o be more precise than at present. We may indeed have been
ited in the measurement of outcome since primitive times, but our
s of what constitutes appropriate outcome remain primitive in
aspects.

speaker pretended that it is going to be easy. One outcome
re, namely patient satisfaction, illustrates this point perfectly.
patients, as Dr Fitzpatrick reminded the conference, express
tion with their treatment almost regardless of what is done to
How patient satisfaction is assessed, by whom, in what setting
w close to the time of the particular treatment — all affect the
s obtained. There is a problem too in what is included under the
la concept 'patient satisfaction'. There is a need to distinguish
n patients' satisfaction with the technical aspects of diagnosis and
int and their satisfaction with the interpersonal care (so-called
ing') that they receive. Once again some helpful signposts were
ed to help progress. Robert Maxwell's six variables relating to
lity of a particular aspect of a health service — access, relevance
, effectiveness, equity, efficiency and social acceptability — have
ication here too. Indeed, the issue of social acceptability, of a
lar treatment for example, is largely patient satisfaction under
name.

vice interested in outcome should be anxious to develop
s of patient satisfaction that take account of the substantial
s inhibiting patients from expressing dissatisfaction. Here and
roughout the controversy flitted the heretical thought that
the nature of the National Health Service, with its lack of
tion, militated against a professional interest in patient
ion. Were not patients fortunate to be treated at all, and so
The emphasis placed in the private sector on the attractiveness
nical setting, on what might be termed the 'perks' of clinical
reminds us of the importance of patient satisfaction to
s and organisations who depend on patient goodwill for their
d.

rse here is the rub, and not a few participants in the conference
v to point it out. The satisfied patient may well be satisfied with
e. Did we not all know physicians with substantial private
and a clientele of adoring patients but to whom we fellow
is, with our insiders' knowledge, would not send our dog? A

9 | Some conclusions

Anthony W. Clare
Trinity College, Dublin, and St Patrick's Hospital, Dub

The most obvious conclusion to be drawn from t
at the end of the day's proceedings, it was very r
argue that the medical profession has really take
establish how the outcome of many of its intervent
and how appropriate many of these treatments ar
conference had opened with a calm reminder fron
that doctors have always been interested in
Treatment trials of one kind or another bear witn
of medical practitioners to establish exactly how
surgical operation is in a given clinical situatio
some might well have been forgiven for wonderi
been about. Since investigations and treatn
medicine can be time-consuming and expensive
doctor interested to determine their effectivene

Professor Rosser soon established, and a suc
to re-state it again and again, that most doctors
have had a somewhat simplistic notion of outcon
observed, some physicians working with elderl
the conclusive test of suitability for discharge a
walk unaided to the toilet. It is not just a ques
QALY road we should all go, but rather how w
outcome measures that are of importance an
into a schema alongside traditional outcome
remission and restoration of function. Of cours
is no great problem. As Professor Rosser point
so deplorable that any intervention cannot fai
tial change on, for example, the health disabil
anxious to remind her audience of a fact that
difficulty in appreciating, namely that certa
worse than death and any clinical interventio
impact save the unnecessary prolongation of

good bedside manner might produce high levels of patient satisfaction but yield abysmal levels of therapeutic outcome. The answer to this too recurred like a Wagnerian motif: the assessment of patient satisfaction is only one element, albeit an important one, in the overall assessment of patient outcome.

Doctors' traditional indifference to patients' views may in part be due to a suspicion arising from the seeming subjectivity of it all. The assessment of pain is a case in point. Dr McQuay's suggestion (such a simple yet radical one) that pain should be assessed routinely in every patient, alongside blood pressure, pulse and temperature, reminded us of the central significance of pain to patients and its neglect by doctors. But assessment of pain need not be entirely subjective: the extent to which a patient is disabled by pain can to a considerable extent be established objectively.

Given that there are problems surrounding the assessment of outcome in individual patients, they pale alongside the problems of assessing the output of health services. How near are we to agreement on what constitutes an appropriate outcome? Dr Brook, adopting a challenging stance befitting a member of the Rand Corporation, and with his tongue not entirely in his cheek, fired off a number of suggestions. Could we do with a Michelin guide to hospitals which might mention such things as death rates from certain surgical interventions? Should every randomised trial include an appropriately detailed measure of health status? Colleges like the Royal College of Physicians could cease awarding memberships and fellowships for life, and instead require recipients to provide an ongoing and verifiable commitment to postgraduate education, research and outcome assessment. Perhaps there should be an expansion of the consensus conference concept whereby respected medical experts together arrive at norms, goals, objectives of diagnosis, management and treatment which might serve as yardsticks in the measurement of good practice. (The King's Fund in Britain has already initiated a number of such conferences; issues discussed include the effectiveness of breast cancer screening, coronary artery bypass surgery and the management of stroke.)

The spectre of self-governing hospitals introduces an urgency into the debate on accreditation. Other countries, most notably the United States and Australia, have adopted quite elaborate procedures relating to optimal standards for health care facilities. The advantages, as spelled out by Dr Roberts, might appear conclusive. The problem is that accreditation can be expensive and time-consuming, and it can slowly degenerate into a sterile exercise, a bureaucratic routine. However, the establishment of minimum standards, not merely for hospitals but for other community-based facilities, becomes well-nigh irresistible once the NHS monopoly is discarded in favour of a market-oriented, competitive model of service delivery.

The major conclusion is that it is indefensible to avoid measures of outcome and to rely on measures of output (the present NHS position) merely because outcomes are difficult to assess and the tools are either lacking or remarkably crude. The outcome measures may indeed be crude, indirect and imprecise but, as Leyshon has argued,[1] if we use them more 'we can improve the quality of service to people in our communities until better and more direct measurements become available'. Indeed, when we look at the crude measures — mortality statistics — it is clear that there is much to be done. Less attention is given to avoidable causes of death by Britain than by other Western countries. The picture gained from looking at mortality from serious conditions is no less gloomy. Such variability in mortality outcome is more than matched by variability in medical practice. Payer[2] reminds us that it may be even more complicated than that. Consider her discussion of cosmetic breast surgery. As judged by the sale of bras, the average breast size in the United States of America is identical to that in France, yet the commonest plastic surgical operation in the US is breast augmentation whereas in France it is breast reduction. Also, contemplate the difficulties in making sense of outcome measurement in the treatment of hypotension which in Germany is one of the commonest cardiovascular conditions diagnosed whereas in the UK it is not regarded as a disorder at all.

This leads me to a conclusion derived not so much from what any speaker said at this absorbing conference but from the speaker who was not there — the medical anthropologist. Throughout there appeared an implicit consensus that we all knew what we were talking about when it came to disorder. There might be remarkable differences in treatment approaches, symptom measurement and diagnostic procedures adopted, but the central target of our deliberations appeared clearly defined and in focus. In fact, and it is what makes the assessment of patient satisfaction such a minefield, the boundaries of disease are very ill-defined, and one of the most potent factors shaping and distorting them is cultural. Why do prostatectomies, hysterectomies, cardiovascular operations and appendicectomies vary to a remarkable degree from one area to another within a country and from one country to another? Why are rates of hospital admission, investigative procedures, laboratory tests and physician visits so highly variant? Physician visits occur on average 15 times per patient per year in Israel, 10 times in Germany, 4 to 5 times in the UK and the US, and 2 to 3 times in Scandinavia. Obviously factors such as the availability of medical resources and facilities, payment and reimbursement mechanisms play a role, and they are much studied, but the social background and attitude of the patient and the cultural forces shaping the health care system may be equally or perhaps even more influential.

So a final conclusion might be that a comprehensive discussion of the issue of medical outcome needs to include the medical anthropologist if we are to avoid slipping into the assumption that our notions of disease have a scientific precision and objectivity lacking in our therapeutic responses and our health care systems. The assessment of outcome is too important to be left to clinicians, and certainly too subtle to be left to health economists, administrators and epidemiologists. Indeed, as this conference made clear, it cannot be left to any one group because it affects us all — politicians, professionals and the public.

References

1. Leyshon, G.E. (1987) What is quality? In *Creating quality in the NHS*. Occasional Papers No. 11. Centre for Professional Development, Department of Community Medicine, Manchester Medical School.
2. Payer, L. (1989) *Medicine and culture*. London: Gollancz.